Orphan of War

From Ukraine To Canada

By Way Of World War II

A memoir by

Lesia Popadenko Hawrelak

For Bill,
with best wishes!

Lesia

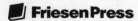

FriesenPress

Suite 300 - 990 Fort St
Victoria, BC, Canada, V8V 3K2
www.friesenpress.com

ISBN
978-1-4602-6529-1 (Paperback)
978-1-4602-6530-7 (eBook)

1. Biography & Autobiography, Cultural Heritage

Distributed to the trade by The Ingram Book Company

FOR MY THREE DAUGHTERS WHO BRING ME JOY

Tamara (Tammy), Katherine (Kathy), Jennifer (Jen)

INTRODUCTION

In 2004, my granddaughter, Alexis, was a grade five student. Her class was discussing Anne Frank and World War II survivors. When Alexis told her teacher that her grandmother was a survivor, I was asked to come to class and talk about my experiences during the war. I agreed and decided to make the children envision the difference between their lives and my life when I was the same age.

In my half hour presentation, I introduced my family, my old country of Ukraine, and my experiences in the war and later in refugee camps. I talked about the effects of war on people trapped in the war zone and the impacts it had on me personally.

I was surprised at how involved and interested the children were in the discussion that followed. The teacher suggested that I write my memoirs because it is important to study history through personal experiences. I had not realized it was as captivating and traumatic as it was until I began sharing with others. This was my life, my memories. It's what I know.

So, for the next eight years I was trying to compose my manuscript. I wrote, rewrote, added, deleted, and mostly ignored it for months at a time until 2012. When it was finally completed, I found it was very difficult for me to expose my private and personal adventures, feelings, thoughts, and beliefs to the public. Once again I decided to put my manuscript away, overlooking the fact that it was ready for self-publishing.

During the entire year of 2014, however, the world was watching the injustice imposed by the Russian Government upon Ukraine and Ukrainian people. The intimidation and lies from Moscow in the twenty-first century brought back memories for me about Russian brutality and murder during my childhood. It was time for me to publish my memoirs.

The story of my life is set against the backdrop of Europe during World War II. It includes several historical events and people who suffered under Stalin's and Hitler's brutality. After the war, some of us were fortunate to immigrate to Canada because we were afraid to return to our native Ukraine where imprisonment or even death awaited us under Stalin's powerful Soviet dictatorship.

Everything I have written is true to the best of my memories and my knowledge. Over the past seventy years, I have acquired knowledge of historical events by reading books, attending classes, listening to the media, and interacting with older people who have lived through similar experiences. Some facts come from my mother's letters, notes and photographs, but my memories shall remain with me forever. I begin with the first recollection of living in Ukraine as a very young child and continue describing my story for nearly fifty years of my existence.

I have not collaborated with anyone for accuracy of my facts and have not changed any names of the persons mentioned. The opinions expressed here, including any errors, are entirely my own and I believe them to be true.

CHAPTER I

Early Life in Ukraine

When I think back to my earliest childhood of being approximately three or four years of age, I am delighted to remember those first, happy, carefree, beginnings. I was born in Zhytomyr, 130 kilometers west of Kyiv (the capital of Ukraine) to a wonderful Ukrainian family. I lived in a luxurious apartment with my mom, dad, and an older sister. They loved me very much and created a secure, enjoyable environment in which to grow up. My dad was a professor and my mom a teacher. They met at a university in Zhytomyr when Mom was a student and Dad was her instructor. During that period, a romance flourished between them and, in 1933, they were married. Two years later, my sister Halia (short for Halyna) was born.

Mom and dad married in 1933.

I came into the world almost three years after my sister was born. My parents named me Olesia, and my nickname was Dzyoun. In our comfortable home, we always had a nanny who lived with us and took care of my sister and me because mom started teaching right after her graduation. I enjoyed everything in those happy days and especially loved going to the beach and on picnics.

On the beach; Halia and me, dad and mom with nanny and friend in 1940.

There was one thing I objected to in those early days though. It was the fact that I was smaller and younger than my sister. I wanted to be more like Halia who was already going to school in grade one, so I would make our nanny put my sister's clothes on me. I thought that it would make me look older and smarter.

With love and contentment surrounding me, I had all the benefits of a normal happy childhood. My sister and I were taught to be polite, pleasant, and respectful to older people.

4

Our nanny with Halia and me wearing Halia's clothes.

I remember always having to curtsey and smile every time I was introduced to grownups. Friends of our family would say that my sister and I were the lovely daughters of Professor Olexa Makarowich Popadenko and Tamara Antonovna Baranowska (mom's maiden name).

Mom in grey fur coat with university friends in 1939.

I loved my mom. Before bedtime she would tell me stories about fairies and butterflies. She would sing Ukrainian songs to put me to sleep. But dad was my favourite in those days. He used to whisper to me that I was his precious little girl and called me *Moye zolotko* (a Ukrainian term of endearment). He would always cuddle me daily. After each meal, he would also congratulate me on my good eating habits with a kiss. He would insist that I lie down for a few minutes after eating so my body continued building strength. I liked being daddy's favourite person and reveled in his never ending attention. He was the most important person to me and I loved him dearly.

Dad at home in 1940.

With my life at its best, I had no idea of the conditions under which Ukrainian people lived in our own land. I was little and my parents protected me from what was happening outside our home, although there were times I heard them talk about the injustice of oppressive conditions that were imposed by the powerful Russian government. In my later years, I learned about that injustice because Eastern Ukraine had become a prison for Ukrainian people. We lived in Eastern Ukraine which belonged to Soviet Russia while Western Ukraine was under Polish occupation. Both rulers of Western and Eastern Ukraine administered an authoritarian form of government where Ukrainian culture and language were repressed. It was even worse for us because the Soviet totalitarian regime insisted upon complete Russification (conversion of non-Russians to accept Russian ways and language, thus increasing their empire). Every aspect of human life was controlled from the Kremlin in Moscow. It came under the authority and concern of Stalin's Communist Party, which resulted in torture and even death if one was labeled as an "enemy of the people". Stalin originated the concept "enemy of the people", making it possible to use cruel methods of punishing innocent people. My parents were aware of such tyranny and, being teachers, they knew how and when to use both Ukrainian and Russian languages, which did not cause any overt threat to the dictatorial control of the Russian administration. I remember that inside our home we all spoke Ukrainian but on the street in public we spoke Russian. The official language in schools, business, theatre, and the press was strictly Russian. Thus, Ukrainian history and its people could be concealed as Russia's quest to destroy Ukraine's existence as a separate, distinct country continued.

Going back to my childhood of innocence, I was unaware of such severity and brutality under which Ukrainian citizens lived in Ukraine. Even before I was born, Ukrainians endured cruelty under Russian domination. First it began with the Tsarist times and then, much worse, during the Communist Party with both Lenin and Stalin at its head. From Ukraine's perspective, Stalin was the most evil dictator. He was on a mission to wipe out any notion of Ukrainian independence and used inhuman methods of destruction. He wanted to demonstrate to Ukrainian citizens that he was their supreme ruler. In 1932-33, he created a man-made famine *Holodomor*, which starved millions of people to death. Stalin confiscated farm land from its owners and took away all private ownership of land and property by creating *kolhosp* (forced collective property and collective farms). Farmers had to work hard from morning to night and remain hungry because they were not allowed to keep any harvest for their own use. Everything was to be delivered to the government under strict supervision. If anyone kept any bits for themselves, they could be executed, although the majority of people were left to die slowly of starvation. More than seven million Ukrainian peasants were starved to death, one third being children. For Ukrainians, this massacre was what the Holocaust was to the Jews. Thankfully, on May 29, 2008, (the 75th anniversary of the *Holodomor*), the Canadian Federal Government recognized *Holodomor* as a man-made genocide and designated the fourth Saturday of each November to be commemorated as the Memorial Day for millions of its victims.

In my adult life in Canada, I personally met people who survived such cruel treatment and told stories of how they had to turn to eating gophers to stay alive. Mr. Chernetski of Calgary, one of the survivors, now deceased, would say that living in Canada he could not kill a gopher because he never forgot that eating them saved his life. Other stories I heard from the survivors were about the children who would go into the fields searching for any leftover ears of grain. When spotted, they were shot dead right on sight. It is incomprehensible that leaders of the free world did nothing to arrest this inhumanity, but that could certainly be attributed to the Soviet propaganda. Stalin's evil government was brilliant in portraying Soviet Ukraine as a well-fed place. Ukraine was called the Bread Basket of Soviet Union which made it easier for Stalin to deceive the West. Disgracefully, an American reporter, who was based in Moscow at the time, misled the world by repeating Soviet lies that in 1932-33 there was no famine in Ukraine. Thus, Stalin was able to make a point to all that his assurance for collectivization was good for his people and that it was a necessary contribution towards his great plans for future industrialization which required maximum capital.

Because Stalin's repression of Ukrainian culture and nationalism by killing off such a large number of peasants in 1932-33 did not work, he turned to Ukrainian intelligentsia, educated people like my parents who also believed in liberty and justice. He made very sure that anyone showing any Ukrainian consciousness appeared as a political threat and was dealt with by harsh punishment of hard labour and shipped to Siberia. Such punishment would be achieved by making up some false form of crime committed by the innocent Ukrainian persons, just to ensure they were removed permanently. My mother and my father, who loved their Ukrainian identity, had to be discreet about saying anything that would jeopardize our safety.

World War II began in 1939 with Hitler's invasion of Poland. During these alarming conditions, my own perfect world, which I remembered so fondly, came to an abrupt end in late 1941. Everything drastically changed for me. Suddenly, without any warning, my daddy was gone from us. He was taken away from our home and forced to join the Red Army of Russian soldiers to fight the Germans in World War II. At the time, I did not know the meaning of war and its destruction of human life. All I knew was that my beloved daddy disappeared and I missed him very much. But, there was more to come for my dire awareness later. With daddy's departure, our nanny was gone too and mom said that we had to leave our comfortable place immediately. She told us that it was no longer safe to live in Zhytomyr because many citizens were disappearing without any warning, just like our daddy and our nanny. So, my mother, my sister, and I headed directly for the train station to go to Kyiv where mom had some friends. With no time to pack, we took one suitcase filled with a few pieces of clothing, mom's literary papers, and pictures which she always kept with her. Most of our things were left behind and that's when I found myself thrown into a completely new lifestyle where the joys and the fun I had experienced in the past were now all gone.

The train station was full of noisy people and screaming was heard throughout the inside and outside of the train. People were in fear of being caught by Soviet Russians or by Nazi Germans who were already fighting on the soil of Ukraine. They fled in different directions in search of safety, just as we did. When we boarded the train, I saw a heavy set woman grabbing her husband and, as she sat down, she pulled her wide skirt up over his head and tried hiding him under it. My sister and I thought it was pretty funny at the time, but the humour did not last long because the man was spotted and pulled away, while the woman cried hysterically for him. This was her way of trying to protect her loved one from being captured because both Stalin's Russians and Hitler's Germans were snatching Ukrainians for army recruitment or for forced labour camps or even death.

We arrived in Kyiv within two hours and settled in a small one-room apartment. Although it was tiny, it had a piano in a corner of the room and one bed for all three of us. Halia was glad to see a piano because she could already play. Mom assured us it was safe for the time being to stay there. How safe? It appeared that it would be safe from the Russians because the Germans had already moved into Kyiv and promised Ukrainian citizens to get rid of Soviet brutality. They even dropped flyers from planes assuring the opening of Ukrainian schools, press, theatre, all to restore freedom from Russia. Ukrainians always hoped for such a miracle but, unfortunately, Hitler's promise did not come to fruition and things did not improve. Ukrainians should have realized that Hitler and Stalin were both just as evil. Life continued to be difficult for us in Kyiv and in a very short time things got even worse. Because of the influx of Germans using Ukraine as their source of food, it left a shortage of anything to eat for other people and we were becoming very hungry. I remember an incident about our cupboard where bread was stored. The day the shelf was empty, mom was searching for traces of bread crumbs, for that was all we would have to eat. The next day, mom went out and, when she came back home, we noticed her very short hair. My sister and I said,

"What happened to your beautiful long hair, mom?"

"Oh, I just cut if off and traded it for this lovely bread," she responded.

The bread was rationed and had to last for a long time. I hated being so hungry but what was even worse was my daddy's absence. My mom had heard that he was sent to fight the Nazi Germans somewhere in Poland. Other than that we had no news. We missed him very much and were waiting to hear from him. Every day I hoped for daddy's return and kept asking mom how soon it would be.

The day finally arrived when mom received news about dad. The news was something we did not expect. It was in a form of a note stating that dad was killed in action in Poland and there were no survivors from his whole unit of soldiers. We were all in shock and I could not believe that my daddy was dead. I kept thinking,

Not my daddy. Not my daddy who loved me as his precious little girl and who I loved with all my heart, he cannot be gone from me forever. I want him back!

For the rest of that day we all cried and mom tried to comfort me and my sister. She tried to explain to us that we were in the war where horrible things happened to good people. Being a small child, about four and a half years old, I could not understand any of it except for the fact that everything changed for us. I remember being filled with grief and frustration for losing my daddy and I remember hating my new life of poverty, hunger, and danger.

Our last family photo; mom, my sister, me and dad in 1941.

CHAPTER II

Surviving World War II

Our stay in that little room in Kyiv did not last long because something very unexpected and interesting happened. Occasionally, mom would leave my sister and me in the room to go out and attend secret meetings. These secret meetings were held with friends who were Ukrainian teachers, writers, artists, and all those Stalin tried to eliminate by wanting to turn Ukraine into Russia. I later found out the meetings discussed Stalin's inhuman acts and the need to find a way for Ukrainians to preserve their national identity, despite Russia's evil control from Moscow. During one such meeting, a Ukrainian visitor, who had just escaped from a Siberian labour camp, arrived to talk about his experiences in Siberia and about the current situation affecting Ukrainians in their own country. This visitor was a true Ukrainian patriot, a professor, and a writer, whose whole family suffered under Stalin's evil campaign of terror. He lost his own father to Stalin's man-made famine in Ukraine during 1932-33 and he himself endured nearly four years in a Siberian labour camp working on railroad construction. This man was an innocent victim of Russia's evil destruction of Ukrainian identity where he was wrongly sentenced as a political prisoner and labeled an "enemy of the people". His name was Mykola Prychodko.

Unbeknownst to me then, mom had listened to the visitor's stories and was very impressed with the vast knowledge this person had about the dreadful existence of the political situation for Ukrainian people. She heard him confirm that Stalin was worried about Ukrainian national traits existing in his Soviet Union of Russian domination. Prychodko said that Stalin and his cronies in the Kremlin were trying to turn Ukrainians into "Little Russians" by giving us an identity as the second class citizens, thus, proclaiming Ukrainian language a Russian peasant dialect, forbidding it to be spoken. With threats and destruction of Ukrainian educational institutions, they banned Ukrainian books and rewrote historical events making contents full of Soviet lies. In my own studies in Canada, I explored this issue and discovered that on the international scene, Stalin was successful in concealing Ukraine's true history in order to glorify his Great Russia. For example, I read Russian chronicles where historical details of the medieval times were misrepresented. I found statements referring to the ancient land of Rus as the land called Russia and claiming the city of Kyiv as the city of Russia, ignoring Ukraine's significance during that special period. Truthfully, Rus was the ancient land around Kyiv on Ukraine's territory encompassing Russia to the Northeast and Belorus to the North. Kyiv was a powerful Ukrainian city benefiting all three East Slavic states of Kyivan Rus. Historically, Ukraine was a country whose culture and people had a strong love of freedom being influenced and aspired by ways of Western Europe, whereas Russia possessed hostile tendencies towards the West.

When mom's secret meeting ended, she continued thinking about the visitor and about his suffering in Siberia. She got home, got ready for bed, as my sister and I were already asleep, and with the lights turned off, she saw an unexplained vision. It was a moving skeleton of a man in the dark corner of the room by the piano. The skeleton resembled the new visitor, Mykola Prychodko, who appeared in the shadow of the room and slowly began approaching her. She got so startled, she jumped into bed between my sister and me, waking us up. She couldn't understand why he appeared as a ghost and frightened her. However, a few years later, I heard mom say that it made more sense to her when she recalled that omen.

That scary experience of the ghost stayed with mom because she was the type of person who believed in supernatural powers. One time I overheard her telling someone that when she was a university student, she had a similar experience of a strange apparition. Her best friend, who had moved away, showed up one evening when mom was studying. Mom said that her friend arrived and, being between trains with some free time to spend, wanted to visit mom before catching the next train. They talked, drank tea, and after a short visit together, the friend left. The next morning, mom received a telegram that her friend had been killed the day before. Some might question my mom's vision of her deceased friend or interpret it as a dream after falling asleep from studying hard at night, but she was sure of its reality and was truly convinced that her friend was with her as there was proof in the two empty cups of tea. In those early years of my life, I also believed in the spiritual world and, although I was never afraid of gangsters or thieves or any other bad people, I was always afraid of the things that I could not understand. It could be something like a ghost entering my room through the wall or a scary thing under the bed that would crawl out and grab me and, of course, all that would occur during the dark night. My fear also resulted from more scary stories that I had heard others tell alongside my mom's, and these would always keep turning around in my little head. I remember one story a man was telling us about the time he lived in an old house that gave off crying sounds from the attic. Every night, he heard small footsteps and a child crying above his bed. Finally, he decided to go up and see for himself. Before crawling up there, he made a cross from twigs tied together, to ensure personal safety. At midnight he was in the attic and, sure enough, a ghost of a youngster was visible to him. He pointed the cross at the child and said,

"I baptize you in the name of the Father, the Son, and the Holy Ghost. You shall be named…."

I do not remember the name this man said. Following that night, there were no more noises. This man also told that, a year later, the old house was being demolished for road improvement and a grave of a small child was found under the house. I did not like hearing such stories and became even more paranoid of ghosts and especially of the dark. I was taught to believe the spiritual world was part of our real world and was encouraged to listen to my guardian angel for decision making by rejecting the desires of the devil. For me, the angel was always sitting on one shoulder while the devil was on the other and it was up to me to make the right choices. The nicest part about my angel was that I always knew it would protect me from harm. There were many times when I was afraid of something, I would talk to my guardian angel and it would make me feel better. Every night, I always knelt beside my bed, crossed myself, and prayed for the safety ahead and for the protection of my family, including my daddy in heaven.

In spite of mom's scary vision/dream of Mykola Prychodko, which she experienced after that first secret meeting, she continued spending time with him and with their mutual friends. Soon they hit it off and started dating. Mom was a widow with two children and he was single again after divorcing his first wife. Apparently, when he was sent to prison in Siberia, his wife gave him up for good. Both mom and Prychodko were patriotic to their Ukrainian roots and had the same beliefs and hopes for liberation of Ukraine. In no time they were married and he adopted my sister and me as his children. So now we became a new family. My name was changed from Popadenko to Prychodko. Although I had my stepfather's name, I felt no paternal nurturing like my daddy and rarely interacted with him. My new stepdad also didn't like mom's name, Tamara, because it was associated with Russian names, so he began calling mom Oksana, though her official name remained Tamara. This stepfather was a respected, knowledgeable, educated individual who was admired by many people. My mother also was an intelligent, educated, respected woman likewise admired as much as her husband. Together they involved themselves with other Ukrainian intellectuals and attended many secret meetings, some of which were held at our own residence.

Mom with knee bandage, stepdad on the right behind her with friends in 1942.

In the beginning of their marriage, everything seemed pleasant and normal. I don't know how it was possible, but my living conditions vastly improved after mom's marriage. We moved from that one-room place into a bigger apartment which had a small balcony overlooking a row of chestnut (*kashtany*) trees on Pankiwska Street in the heart of Kyiv. I have no idea how my stepdad was able to provide us with such comfortable accommodation, but it may have been the residence belonging originally to his friends; a physician and his wife who vacated the lovely place when the Germans arrived in Kyiv. The apartment had two bedrooms, a dining room with a long table and a chandelier hanging above it.

Slowly I started liking my more comfortable lifestyle, except for the fact that my stepdad was nothing like my real daddy, whom I still missed very much. My stepfather was charming and likeable but, unfortunately, I do have a memory of a bad incident during a family argument. It happened when I saw him push my mom while in their angry state of disagreement. Even though I did not know what was happening, I had become furious and decided that I must protect my mother. I grabbed a wooden coat hanger and was going to hit him with it. I said,

"Don't you hurt my mom or I'll kill you."

He gently took the hanger away from me and told me to go to bed. Although I was only about five or six years old, I was not afraid to retaliate to what I assumed was his bad behaviour. Unfortunately, what followed was our mutual dislike for each other. Sadly, for the rest of my life we never formed any kind of closeness. His attitude towards my sister was quite different because he really liked her. I guess I don't blame him for preferring my sister over me. Everyone loved her. Everyone said she was a perfect child. She was beautiful, talented, adorable, and very polite. I, on the other hand, was less liked. At times I would not listen to mom or do everything that was expected of me, and mom would say,

"Why can't you be more like Halia? Look how polite she is and how everyone likes her?"

That's when I would think that mother must like Halia more than me, and would wish that my daddy was still alive. I knew dad loved me best. He used to make me feel that I was the most important person in the whole world. Such feelings of being second best to my sister lasted only during the times I was being disciplined for something I did wrong. Other than that, I appreciated having a wonderful, older sister like my Halia. I loved her very much. I was aware that she was beautiful and talented because she could play piano brilliantly and excel in sports. I, on the other hand, just wanted to be loved. And to the outside world, we were two lovely sisters with big bows in our hair.

Halia and me.

19

We could not stay in Kyiv. It was 1943 and the Germans were not resurrecting Ukraine's independence as promised. Instead, they were capturing thousands of Ukrainians to work as slaves in their factories and crematories. At the same time, the Russians continued forcefully arresting citizens to add as troops for their Red Army. Ukrainians were in the middle of these two evil forces; Hitler with the Nazis and Stalin with the Soviets, both bent on destruction of human life. Their drive for world domination resulted in equal wickedness where both slaughtered innocent people in millions; murder and genocide was on both sides. Both got rid of corpses with the indignity of mass graves. Although Hitler's priority was to eliminate all Jews and Gypsies (Roma), he also enslaved and killed Ukrainians whom he called subhuman beings *untermenschen.* Stalin equally tortured and killed people at his whim because anyone who was disliked by him or his cronies in the Kremlin was labeled as an enemy and traitor to mother Russia. Today, we can find additional information about the brutality of Hitler and Stalin. It all started when both were on the same side. Both rulers were dictators who aimed to expand their respective empires. As early as 1939, both were partners in crime signing a Soviet-Germany non-aggression pact to discuss mutual plans for capturing Eastern Europe between them. Even in 1940, Stalin was with Hitler when Auschwitz concentration camp opened. But in 1941, to Stalin's surprise, Hitler turned against him and invaded the USSR land. Thus, Stalin became Hitler's enemy and was determined to destroy him and win the war.

Living within such fearful surroundings of Nazi and Soviet fighting, people were running away, leaving most of their belongings behind because of the possibility of arrest to join an army or to be deported to forced hard labour. It was especially dangerous for my stepdad to remain in Kyiv, so we decided to escape westward together with other evacuees. We were lucky to get on the last truck taking people west. We boarded with many others, sitting closely together in the back of an open truck. We travelled until we reached the town of Rivne in Western Ukraine. It's not clear how long we stayed in Rivne but I do remember that before we left Rivne for Lviv, I got a new dress that mom sewed by hand using pieces of cloth from an old sweater and some old corduroy pants because I needed something larger and warmer to wear. It was also the time when I had my hair cut short because I had lice and mom thought it would be easier to get rid of them with short hair. She tried combing the lice out and also killed them by squeezing them with her finger nails right on my scalp. As she squished the lice, her fingers turned red from the blood.

Halia and me in my new dress and short hair in 1943.

Our trip to Lviv was by passenger train. I sat quietly next to mom who put her arm around me and clutched our suitcase with her other hand. My stepdad sat close to my sister and kept the second suitcase near him. These two suitcases and the clothes on our backs were all our worldly possessions. With the train's speed increasing and the sun setting beyond the horizon, we were slowly falling asleep to the quiet humming of the train engine. In no time, the night turned very dark and complete silence penetrated throughout the cabins. Then, suddenly to our surprise, the sky became very bright, lit up like a sunny day, and the sound of airplanes was heard above us. Flares (*rakety*) were shot from the planes making the sky very clear and visible. The train stopped in the middle of nowhere. Immediately bombs began falling on the train. Confusion and riots among passengers created great commotion with loud screams throughout the train. People were trying to get off by pushing one another. My mother grabbed my hand and pulled it with all her strength. She dragged me off the train, while my stepfather was pulling my sister off. In the middle of all the bombing and screaming, we were able to jump off into a field together with a few other fortunate people. Once on the ground, we ran for our lives not knowing where we would end up, leaving behind the bombs, the explosions, the noise, the burning of everything and everyone. We kept running and running further away from the blasting and screaming noises of the train wreck. As I ran, the pain in my arm from being dragged was excruciating. The ground under my feet was damp and slippery and the tall grass was hitting and hurting my face. I don't know how far or how long we ran, but eventually we spotted an underground dugout. This gave us an opportunity to hide in it and, hopefully, remain safe.

We stayed in the dugout for the rest of the night. The dugout was cold and it's a good thing it was not a bitter winter season with severely cold weather. Inside was a wooden floor and a wooden door that did not close but at least it provided us with an opportunity to have some rest. In the morning, we began our search for safety, having become refugees trying to avoid capture by either Russians or Germans in our own land of Ukraine.

To be able to reach a place of safety, we faced many difficulties, mainly because we were using bicycles for our transportation. I don't know how we got those bicycles but somehow we were in possession of a number of them and the four of us plus a few other people were able to reach an empty house. To get there we had to cross a river. I remember being very scared sitting on the front handlebars with an adult male pedaling the bike. I can't remember who he was but I do remember my bum being very sore and I was afraid of falling, especially when we were with bikes in the water. We attempted to cross the river several times because of a very strong current. We would start from the river bank into the water and, before we got half way across, the current would pull us down and we'd have to return to the bank. We made many attempts before we located a spot where we successfully crossed to the other side. The whole experience made me very afraid of water and I hated being so cold and so wet. I thought we would surely drown. Finally, when we reached the other side of the river, trudging through pouring rain, we were able to get to a house where the four of us got a room all to ourselves. This room was in the basement of the house which had one small window overlooking a lovely garden. Once inside from the rain, I looked out the little window and could hear the raindrops sound like dancing footsteps. I could smell the aroma of wet trees and grass. Sometimes, even today, I can still recall that lovely smell of fresh dew when it rains. Although the room itself was chilly and quite dark, it did have a bed and all four of us could gladly curl up in it to keep warm. For sleeping arrangements at night, my sister and I would lie at the feet of stepdad and mom, head to feet style. I remember one night I woke up and heard mom whisper,

"Not now Mykola, the girls could wake up."

"Oh, don't worry, they're sound asleep," was his final answer.

I became very scared because he thought I was asleep when I was already wide awake. So, lying with my eyes closed, I didn't move, and quietly listened to the noises until finally my stepdad got off my mom and silence filled the room once again.

We had to leave that room after a few days as it was time to jump on a train and get further west. The day we were leaving, I was still lying in bed when the others were already up. I wanted to stay in that bed because I was warm in it and the room was cold. I looked up at the ceiling where the light bulb was hanging on a string and I started staring at it. Slowly I began imagining the bulb turning into a beautiful doll; a doll all dressed up in lovely clothes; a doll that started to dance. I decided to blink my eyes slightly to make her dance more and more. As I blinked each of my eyes, the doll continued dancing. When I opened my eyes widely, the doll disappeared and again I saw the ugly light bulb swinging from the ceiling. I tried resurrecting the doll again but was unable. She was gone and I wished with all my heart that someday I would have a doll like that to hold in my arms. From that wonderful pretending, I soon became aware of something new right there and then. I realized that my experience with the doll gave me an opportunity to create a dream world. I could do this simply by imagining nice things. That's when I decided to do the pretending again whenever I felt unhappy or sad.

This time the train we had to take was not a passenger train but a bunch of cattle cars. We boarded an open platform of the freight train and, as it gained speed, the strong wind began hitting my face, my head, and blowing inside my clothes, creating the most uncomfortable cold sensation. But besides being so cold, there was something nice about sitting outdoors to see and smell all the pretty fruit trees that passed us by. Before the long ride ended, the train stopped and we were moved into closed boxcars where it was much warmer. With the sliding doors open, this new place had fresh air, but when the doors were shut, the air became stuffy and smelly. I did not like being in the closed boxcar because of the bad smell and the crowded noisy people, so I decided to make myself feel better by looking through the cracks in the floor and counting the wooden ties across the rail tracks until I fell asleep.

The uncomfortable, overcrowded train brought us somewhere to the Carpathian Mountains of Western Ukraine. I am not sure where the rest of the people went from the train, but I do know the four of us arrived at a farm house near the forest. As it turned out, this place was close to where Ukrainian partisans stayed. Because my uncle, mom's brother, Anton Baranowskij, was one of those partisans in the forest, he was able to visit us. Mom loved her older brother very much and was excited to be reunited with him. As days went by, my sister Halia and I remained on the farm while mom, stepdad, and my uncle would leave us to join the partisans. These Ukrainian partisans belonged to the Ukrainian Insurgent Army - *Ukrainska Povstanska Armiya* (UPA), an underground military defense unit of Western Ukraine who did everything possible to free Ukraine from foreign invaders. They tried to save our nation from the oppression of Nazi control by destroying railroads, trains with ammunition, and enemy soldiers. Although Russian partisans existed in Ukrainian forests as well, they were completely different from the Ukrainian partisans of UPA. Ukrainian partisans of UPA fought both the German Nazis and the Russian Soviets.

Halia and I really enjoyed being on that farm. There was food to eat, such as honey on fresh bread and all of the cow's milk one would want to drink. Being a city dweller, I was not at ease with farm animals. There was a cow that chased me and actually pushed me down. This cow was very mean looking and had huge horns. There were also many geese that scared me. They would chase me and try to nip me. The strange thing about those geese was their feeding. They were force fed and I saw a person shoveling food down their throats by holding them very tightly. Each day mom would go to the forest and then return to us. Apparently she was helping out with the wounded partisans but neither I nor my sister knew about it at the time.

Once again we could no longer remain on the farm because of the enemy's closeness and had to find a safer place. My uncle Anton was going to help us do that. He showed up one evening with an army tank that moved on its tracks and we all crawled inside; my mother, stepfather, my sister, and me together with my uncle. It was strange being inside as it began to move. We were very crowded and I couldn't see out. Soon we stopped and my sister and I were told to remain very quiet because we had to wait for a train to pass. We remained very quiet and waited. After an uncomfortable short period, I heard the sound of an oncoming train and then a huge explosion. Unaware of what created that enormous blast, we later discovered that my uncle had been instrumental in dynamiting railroads and trains carrying ammunition and German soldiers. For me and for my sister, this type of experience did not seem too scary because we felt quite safe with mom, stepdad, and their friends. It seemed more of an inconvenience having to be dragged all over the place and not knowing what would happen next. We, as children, were not aware that we were caught right in the middle of fighting and had to run in every direction to safety, although the adults surely did.

After leaving the farm and its brief delicious food that I enjoyed so much, we continued our journey in the Carpathian Mountains, ending up in a town called Turka. There we celebrated Easter of 1944 and I was almost seven years old. Easter Sunday was a lovely warm day and a group of us were going for a walk. We were about to climb a small hill when my mom stopped walking. She looked at me and at my sister and told us that she wasn't going to go up with us because she was expecting a baby.

It was strange how one minute we were sad and the next happy. One minute safe and the next fearful of what might happen to us. For me, the worst hardships were not having any toys to play with and, at times, wanting more to eat. Aside from that, I was always surrounded by warmth and kindness of friendly, caring people.

Stepdad far left, Halia and me with bows in our hair, a Ukrainian partisan in uniform on the right in 1944.

Those people and my family also gave me the opportunity to develop a respect for my own country, regardless of such difficult times. My parents and my stepdad always instilled a love and admiration for who I was and where I came from. I was also taught that besides the love for our special nation, attainment of education and knowledge was an achievement that could never be taken away from us. I was explained that in war times much can happen, but it was still important to keep the mind active. So my sister and I continued with a form of home schooling that mom and stepdad provided for us whenever it was possible.

A significant thing that was implanted in my childhood and remains with me to this day is pride for my Ukrainian ethnic heritage. Even during all the struggles of war, there was never a time that I rejected or forgot any part of my Ukrainian culture or language among such difficult times.

28

Mom in Ukrainian blouse, Halia and me with bows in our hair held up; celebrating 1944 Easter in Turka.

For example, my love for the sound of a bandura and its beautiful music, introduced to me at very early age, has never left me. This could also be attributed to the fact that I was exposed to it by being in close contact with the members of the Ukrainian National Banduryst Chorus under the direction of Hryhory Kytasty. Those musicians had strong beliefs in human dignity and truth, forced to leave Ukraine because the Soviets wanted to destroy such ideals and had arrested some conductors and singers.

When we were still living in Kyiv, my stepdad, Mykola Prychodko, became involved with them in an administrative capacity and, as a result, I was able to hang around those musicians during most of our travels to safety. This gave me an opportunity to listen to the sounds of the bandura and its lovely heart-warming songs. The bandura is the unique Ukrainian national instrument for Ukrainians as is the bagpipe for the Scots or the balalaika for the Russians. It is like a lute and a harp put together.

29

Young Petro Kytasty with my sister and me in Lviv 1943.

My association with the Capella of the Banduryst members continued, crossing the borders from Ukraine, all the way to Germany. At one of the border stops, I recall a wonderful incident when we were all on a freight train and it stopped somewhere, but I cannot remember where exactly this happened. At the stop, there were ice cream sellers and I remember my stepfather buying me my first ice cream cone. It was the tastiest thing that I had ever eaten. How it was possible to get such a great treat is still not clear to me because I remember seeing German soldiers there as well. It may be that our safety resulted from being with the Bandurysts who had proper German travel documents as musicians. These documents allowed them to perform concerts for the Germans and for the Ostarbeiter camps (Eastern Workers). The Ostarbeiter camps were filled with young Ukrainian imprisoned men and women who were deported from Ukraine by force in order to do hard labour in German factories. There were approximately two million of these young prisoners, kept under strict control, and warned that any attempt to escape would result in death. Such camps are one example of Nazi cruelties that existed for the Ukrainians but it was even worse for the Ukrainian Jewish persons who were singled out for extermination. One of the Nazi notorious killings of Jewish people, as well as some of Ukrainians and Russians, was in Babyn Yar outside Kyiv. Many others were executed in concentration camps like Auschwitz. It is incomprehensible how human beings were killing one another. But among such evils, we can also find compassion and courage towards the suffering of the fellowmen because many Ukrainian families saved many Jewish families by sheltering them from the Germans, despite risking their own personal safety. One of these outstanding, caring people was a Ukrainian Christian who condemned the genocide of Jews. It was Metropolitan Sheptytsky, a Ukrainian Greek Catholic priest. He was credited with saving Jewish children destined for death camps. He smuggled these children to safety by hiding them in monasteries and convents. Recently, on April 24, 2012, the Canadian Government approved a motion in the House of Commons recognizing Metropolitan Sheptytsky for his courageous humanitarian work during World War II. The same time, another wonderful event took place in Canada and the United States. Both countries held a conference of the Ukrainian Jewish Encounter where all different faiths of Ukraine united together to acknowledge the work of Metropolitan Sheptytsky's efforts and, as well, where some of those child Holocaust survivors were present to express their gratitude.

When we finally got to Austria, we settled in some unsightly abandoned camp near Vienna. The place looked repulsive but for the time being it had to be our home. Tall wild grass grew between the dilapidated buildings. The walls inside the buildings were dirty with insulation stuffing jutting out in many places. My sister and I were told never to touch it because its sharpness would cut our hands.

My pregnant mom with stepfather by our buildings in 1944.

One of the things we did there was float on water by sitting on large pieces of wood. That water was created from rain filling big holes which were made from falling bombs. These holes were huge, like craters, and we were cautioned never to play near them because of possible drowning. But, we would still search for boards to float on regardless of the fact that we were forbidden. Personally, I was too scared to get on the water to float so I did not do it but I watched others and my sister doing it.

As desolate as this place was, I did have some fun playing with other kids. Although I was younger than most of them who were more my sister's age, I was allowed to be in their company because I did not reveal what they were doing, like playing in that dangerous water. Another thing we did there was look for cigarette butts to give to our parents. We would find the butts on the road or in the field and bring them home to mom and stepdad. We would watch them remove bits of tobacco and, by ripping the sides of the newspaper where there was no print, they would roll new cigarettes and smoke them.

Crowded conditions inside those ruined buildings were invasive and led to ill feelings for the adults. The adults detested sharing such close quarters with so many people much more than the kids did. There were some bunk beds with no matrasses and many people had to share a bunk bed because there were more people than beds. Everyone desperately tried hanging blankets or whatever they had to separate themselves from other families. Sometimes people would argue or yell and often they would smell. At night, there would be noises such as snoring, coughing, crying, or even laughing. Hanging blankets and any other junk to separate different families in such crammed space did nothing to provide privacy and did nothing to stop noises coming from behind them.

With so many people staying so close to each other, there were things around that children should not get into. I recall the time when my sister and I found a bunch of balloons and tried blowing them up. When my stepdad spotted us, he got angry and took them away, saying that those balloons were to be used as medicinal first-aid for things like sore fingers and thumbs. I couldn't understand his vague explanation until much later I found out from the older kids that those balloons were used by men in order to prevent them from making a baby. In spite of my new knowledge of how babies were made, my mother continued telling me that she found me in a cabbage patch inside a lush vegetable garden in Ukraine.

As days went by, we learned about other things that went on in our camp. One late night when everyone was asleep, my sister and I stayed awake because we had overheard that there was going to be

33

a séance; a meeting to speak to the dead. We had seen a table being built where glue was used instead of nails; a table to be free of metal. We did not know the reason for such odd construction but were anxious to find out for ourselves. We crawled into the top bunk and saw, through the blanket openings, eight people sitting around the constructed table holding hands. The table was covered with paper. On top of the table was a saucer turned upside down with a candle stuck to it. The candle was lit and somebody was spinning the saucer and calling out for some person to answer from the spirit world. My sister and I got really scared and made a noise. Well, that was the end for us. Mom told us to go to sleep and the séance was moved somewhere far away where we could not see or hear anything. Although I was prevented from that scary exposure to such a mysterious ghostly encounter, my fear of the unknown supernatural powers increased even stronger.

World War II continued and to stay safe, we kept moving west until we settled in downtown Vienna. The bombs and air raid sirens occurred every day and night, though it seemed that they blasted mostly at night. Mom gave birth to a baby boy who we called Slavchyk, for Yaroslav. The baby was beautiful but he cried a lot because mom didn't have enough milk to breastfeed him and there was a shortage of food. We did get some powdered milk that came in the form of white cubes and tasted pretty bad. Those cubes had to be dissolved in water before one could drink it. It was easier to drink that stuff for me and for my sister while holding our noses shut because it had a rotten smell. I can't imagine how it tasted for my little brother.

The worst thing for me in Vienna was the air raid sirens and the bombing, especially during the night. It didn't matter where we were. If we were walking down the street and heard a siren, we had to quickly hide somewhere. I remember our walk to a park once. Suddenly, the planes appeared in the sky. We had to jump into a ditch beside the road to hide. Mom tried to protect us by stretching her arms to cover our heads from the sound and the sight of falling bombs. It seemed like a long time for us to remain in such an uncomfortable position. When the planes had finally disappeared, we resumed our walk to the park. The night bombings were the worst. I mostly hated them during the night because I was sound asleep. I had to get up in the middle of the night, get dressed, and run to a bunker (bomb shelter). I can still remember one distinct incident which happened to us when we were in Vienna. It was the middle of the night and I was awakened by my mother. My older sister was already up and my baby brother was screaming in my mother's arms. Mother was trying to hurry me to get dressed so all of us could run down to the bunker. The sound of the sirens was loud and we knew that there was still time to hide from the bombings as long as the sirens were ringing. As soon as they stopped, it was no longer safe to walk out on the street because by that time the planes would be overhead bombing. On this particular night, I decided that I no longer cared about my safety and did not want to get out from a warm bed. I pleaded to be able to stay behind and said,

"Please mom. It's cold and I'm so tired. Please let me stay in bed. I'll be fine on my own and soon you will all be back when the planes are gone."

But, of course, I was not allowed to stay behind. I had to get dressed quickly and then we all ran out of the building. We left everything behind except for the two suitcases always ready to go, filled mostly with our family photos, mother's poetry, and stepfather's manuscripts. When we reached the shelter, we sat there the whole night, waiting impatiently for what would become of us and if we would be saved. Finally the bombing stopped and we were allowed to come out into the open. What I saw outside was shockingly unbelievable. The whole area had become an inferno. There were hardly any buildings left untouched. Most of the buildings were destroyed and everything was an unrecognizable big pile of burning rubble. As we approached the building in which we stayed, we saw that it was completely demolished and still burning. Before anything could be said about my outbursts of wanting to stay behind, my mom took out a metal container, filled it with water, and put a cube of powdered milk into it. She started warming the milk for the baby on the ashes of the fire of our building. My sister and I sat on each of the two suitcases and waited for mom to finish feeding the baby.

One suitcase still with me today.

As difficult as life was for everyone caught up in this lunatic war, there did exist a certain friendship among all those who were struggling to survive under the brutality of both Nazi and Soviet regimes. Besides us, the Ukrainian refugees, there were more other survivors from different ethnic backgrounds such as ordinary Germans, Poles, Russians, Jews, and other human beings abused and fearful just like us. In late 1944, I got very sick and had a problem with my lungs and breathing. Thanks to a German woman, I got better. She ran around looking for some leeches to put on my chest and then also for some sort of glass cups for my back. I can still visualize those ugly huge black leeches on me, and also remember the popping sound when the hot cups were removed from my back. Mom was very worried that I could die because it was later discovered I was suffering from tuberculosis. But the German woman's treatment worked for me. Many other people were also suffering from many different sicknesses. One of our nice young friends had a tape worm. On many occasions, she was given vinegary things to eat and then made to sit on a potty for hours to pass the worm. Her mother was afraid that her daughter was very thin due to the worm that was eating her from inside. I saw this girl sit on the potty many times and was told that the worm would come out but, because a tiny bit would still be left inside, it would grow back again and she would have to repeat the process over and over again.

It didn't matter where we were, alone or shipped with a group of other displaced people, we always tried to be ahead of trouble and always had to make sure we would be safe. Mom used to say that it was dangerous to be on the street in Vienna when spotted by a German soldier or a Gestapo (Nazi political police). Once she did run into a German soldier on the street and, as she tried getting away from him, he grabbed her coat. She was lucky to jump onto a moving street car and get away. When she returned home, she showed us a torn sleeve on her coat. Although mom feared being captured by the Nazis in case she ended up working in their factories, or being caught by the Soviets who searched for their escaped citizens, she was even more worried about the dangerously hungry people that existed among us. This was common knowledge that there were many severely starving people who turned to indulge in human flesh and especially desiring young children. Mom made sure Halia and I were never out of sight from her or from my stepdad and she did not allow us to go outside on our own. I can still remember having my hand held very tightly by mom when walking outdoors. Also, I have not forgotten about our own hunger in those days. At least, occasionally, we were able to find some heavy rye bread and yellow mustard. Actually, I really liked the taste of mustard on bread. But, when this bread was running out, my sister and I overheard my mom and stepdad discussing a plan with three other couples about how they may get some food for all of us. They were proposing a raid on the vegetable farm patrolled by German soldiers. The four women would lure the soldiers into bushes and try keeping them busy while the men, their husbands, would steal some vegetables. I don't remember whether they went through with the plan but I do remember them talking about it. What I also remember is that after my sister and I overheard that discussion, Halia decided to disappear and go looking for some food for all of us on her own. Mom was in a panic when she found Halia missing but, after searching everywhere, Halia was spotted at a farmer's market where she tried to steal food. Halia was not quite ten years old.

Such dreadful living conditions and starvation continued for us among the ruins of Austria until another tragedy happened. Because of shortage of food, improper hygiene, and no medical support, my baby brother died before he could reach his first birthday. I don't have any memory of his funeral and wouldn't be surprised if there wasn't one. Where he was buried is still a mystery to me.

As careful as we were to avoid being captured, we were eventually arrested by the Nazis and herded into a large building with many other people. Inside the building, we were told to have a communal bath to be disinfected and cleaned. At first the men were separated from the women and children. Next, the women and children had to take off all their clothes and shoes and put them neatly in a bundle before entering through a doorway into a large room full of shower heads on the ceiling. On each side of the doorway stood one uniformed German SS guard (Hitler's Protection Squad) holding a shiny thin pointer stick. As we walked through the doorway, those two guards would count us by hitting the stick on our bare bums or breasts or heads. When pretty young women approached the doorway, the guards would take them aside and have them wait, while the rest of us went inside the shower room. Once inside, the heavy doors were bolted. An enormous noise of whimpering and crying followed. Everyone was fearful because they had heard that this could be the place where many people were put to death. No one knew what was going to happen to us. Mom tried to cover my face from looking at the naked women as we all crowded together in the cold, huge room. I had never seen so many naked bodies; old, young, skinny and scary. This was my first communal bathing experience. We stood waiting, all cold, naked, and shivering together, but nothing was coming from the showerheads. Minutes later, which seemed like an eternity, we heard a clatter in the ceiling and everyone became silent. As the clatter increased, the showerheads started pouring out hot water. Instantly everyone burst into laughter and joyful sounds were heard throughout the place. Everyone knew they were safe. I didn't understand the reaction to the hot shower because I didn't know that those showerheads could have sent out gas, instead of water, and killed all of us on the spot. After showering, we did not remain long in that room and were told to get out as soon as possible. We had to put our dirty clothes back on and wait for our documents which were taken away from us before the cleaning ordeal. Much time had passed as we waited to find out what would happen to us next. Meanwhile, some men and women once again were being reunited. After a long wait, it turned out that, according to our documents and the fact that my stepfather could speak a bit of German language, we were dismissed and set free. Amazingly, at that moment, we were actually grateful to the Germans for keeping us away from the Russians who were capturing their own people to torture and slaughter. I wish I could remember where exactly this washing ordeal took place or possibly find more information about this experience among my mother's papers and pictures. Unfortunately, I write only from my memory and have to leave it as is.

What I can still recall clearly is that after our cleaning and examination process, we left Austria by train and arrived in the city of Berlin, Germany sometime during the early spring of 1945. There, we settled in an old building on the second floor. I remember that getting to this building from the train station made me very tired because it was dark and we had to walk a very long distance on messy, littered, cobblestone streets. During our first night in Berlin, we experienced more bombing than anywhere else. And that is how it continued day after day, mostly with nightly attacks, and us running to the bunker for safety. This time my getting to the bunker at night no longer created a problem and I would get out of bed obediently because I had learned my lesson in Vienna where our building was completely destroyed.

Berlin had many enormously sound, efficient, underground bunkers and we were fortunate to have access to one of them. I recall the time we had to enter such a bunker during a raid. The bunker was so big that cars, trucks, and emergency vehicles could drive right inside the bunker. As we entered, we were ushered into a special room after passing through a corridor that led into a hospital area and into some classrooms. This was a huge underworld. We sat down on benches as instructed and could hear the sound of falling bombs above us as well as could see the flickering of lights. We remained sitting quietly and waited. The time we spent there seemed to last for many, many hours and again we wondered if our lives would be spared. When the bombing finally did stop, someone said that sixty-three bombs fell on us from American planes. These bombs destroyed the main entrance of our bunker and blocked it completely. We had to stumble through rooms and hallways until we finally could manage to get outside through the back entrance. Outside we saw everything in ruins; an enormous heap of rubble surrounded by smoke, fire, and dust.

Such destruction, chaos, horror, and agony were part of our nightmare existence for nearly three years, starting in Ukraine and ending in Germany. What occurred next for us was a new hope in believing that maybe all our sufferance of the devastation and the terror we had experienced would stop, because Germany surrendered and World War II finally came to an end. April 30, 1945 Hitler committed suicide in Berlin. May 7-8, 1945 Victory in Europe (VD Day) was joyfully celebrated. Although more than fifty million people lost their lives in the midst of such fighting and torture, our lives were spared and I was almost eight years old.

CHAPTER III

Post War events in Europe

World War II ended but our survival was still questionable. What was going to happen to us as Ukrainian citizens who had ran away from Soviet Ukraine? We left our native country not in search of adventure or prosperity. We left our country because we had to escape from the Soviet tyranny. And now that Stalin became one of the "good guys" who helped save the world from Hitler's cruelty, he got even more power to destroy humanity on the home front. We could not return home to such criminal conditions where this monster in the Kremlin believed that his brutal acts of murdering people were not a crime. A good account of what Ukrainians endured and what was awaiting us upon return under Stalin's regime was published in 1950 in Canada by my stepfather in "Communism in Reality" by N. Prychodko (Winnipeg: New Pathway, p. 8). He wrote,

... Purges are a permanent feature of the Soviet system.... Hundreds of thousands are shipped year after year in barred trains to certain death in Siberia.... Communism brings with it unrestricted police terror, poverty, and the domination of Moscow.

This was the existence that my stepfather had experienced personally in a slave-labour camp in Siberia and he wanted to tell the truth about Soviet rule as it applied to the enslaved nations of the USSR, particularly to Ukraine.

Our unwillingness to return to Soviet Ukraine created a problem for us because we were citizens of Eastern Ukraine, which belonged to the Soviet Union before the war, and Stalin had the right to get us back. He got this authority for collecting all "his" citizens scattered around Europe after the policy of repatriation was approved under the terms of the Yalta Agreement immediately following the victory of World War II. This approval was made by the three powers (America, Great Britain and Russia) dividing the properties among the winners of the war. Stalin was successful in getting all of Ukraine into his USSR, the Western and the Eastern part. However, because Western Ukraine belonged to Poland before World War II, its citizens were not answerable to Stalin's compulsory deportation and had the option of remaining abroad as displaced persons without a country (DPs) or returning home. Our family did not have such an option. We even heard that some Americans befriended the Russians and actually became partners in catching people like us. It was unfortunate that initially Americans believed Russian lies, but at least it did not last long and their hunt soon stopped completely. One other unfortunate fact I came across recently was an old American article describing Soviet Russians in World War II as being loyal to Stalin's leadership and having great respect for the Soviet system. This is quite misleading because many of those Red Army soldiers had been forced to join the army without their own free will; my daddy being one of them. We actually had heard that some of those Russian soldiers even preferred being captured by the Germans. I hope that today, the Western world is much more aware of what really went on inside the USSR territory and how their citizens suffered under Stalin's deception of freedom.

Our only solution to avoid Russia's capture in being sent back to Soviet Ukraine was try to declare a status of becoming DPs from Western Ukraine. These DPs were placed into refugee camps and provided with food and shelter by the United Nations Relief and Rehabilitation Agency (UNRRA) which was created in Germany and Austria right after the war. My mother and stepfather had to find a way to change our birth certificates to show that we were citizens of Western Ukraine.

It was actually quite easy to change our documents because of my stepdad's and mom's connection to the Ukrainian underground activity. Such activity existed for the purpose of freedom and justice during the war and continued for some years later. Our new revised birth certificates, which were processed on legal paper with appropriate dates, places, signatures, and stamps, had the appearance of original documents. They allowed us to legally join other DPs in the barracks of the American Zone in Germany away from Stalin's capture. I think they were altered in Dorfen, just outside Munich, but I am not entirely sure. Thus, the place of my birth became Horodishche, Western Ukraine and no longer my true birthplace of the city of Zhytomyr, Eastern Ukraine. One discrepancy did exist between my baptism and my birth certificate because one had my name as Prychodko and one had Popadenko. An explanation was provided.

Certificate of Olesia (Olexandra) Popadenko. Olesia's mother remarried before Olesia was born. The name of Prychodko appears on the birth certificate. He was her stepfather.

(dated) August 8, 1937
(signed) Theodor Bohatuik, Pastor

Later mom was also saying that our new documents had some inconsistencies with ages as well. She herself seemed to have two different birth dates, 1917 and 1914. My own dates were 1938 and 1937. It seems that the best year for me was chosen to benefit my food rations. Children in refugee camps received different rations of milk and butter according to their ages. We were fed daily through a union kitchen and once per week received those rations. Although I may have been born in 1938, officially, the date for my legal birth certificate was 1937. I have kept this year because it got me into Canada where I have had the opportunity to become a Canadian citizen and live in this wonderful country of socio-economic advantages and true democratic freedom.

Mom between Halia and me, stepdad behind Halia, and friends in Fussen camp in 1945.

Our first refugee camp as Ukrainian DPs was in Fussen, Bavaria. We were finally feeling safe from Stalin's violence and hoped to secure a more peaceful existence.

In Fussen, we lived with some famous Ukrainian personalities. I used to call them uncles. The ones I still remember were Uncle Osmachka, Uncle Bahrianij and Uncle Kytasty, the director of the Ukrainian

Banduryst Chorus. Ivan Bahrianij, a respected political leader and writer, was also a wonderful painter. I recall sitting fatigued for a portrait he painted of me and one of my sister. He also drew a picture for us and called it, "Ukrainian Birds flying home."

Drawing by Ivan Bahrianij in 1946.

For the first time in a long time, I started experiencing some wonderful things in the camp at Fussen. My dreams came true when I got a doll. I don't know exactly how mom was able to get me a doll but, to my joy, she did and I got one all to myself to keep forever. It was a soft doll stuffed with straw and had a hard face. It was dressed in a lovely green dress with a matching bonnet. Mom cut off some of her own hair and glued it to the doll's bold head. I cherished and played with it until eventually some straw began coming out of its arms and legs from too much handling. I still have the doll in its original state and it still has my mother's hair on it. Today, I can touch this doll and examine mom's beautiful black hair, bringing back memories of my beloved mother who I have missed all my life.

My doll with mom's black hair.

Another exciting event that took place in Fussen was my eating the most delicious sweet concoction after a long period of craving sweets. Mom made a special dessert we called Goggle Moggle. It was made with fresh eggs and sugar. Yolks were separated from whites; then yolks were stirred with sugar until almost lemony colour; whites were beaten with a fork until quite stiff; finally both were mixed gently together. If vanilla was available, a drop would go in as well. Such a treat was terrific. I would make it myself for many years to come until eventually I heard that raw eggs should not be eaten and I had to give it up.

The Fussen camp was also the place where I began my childhood immunization and have kept some records of it.

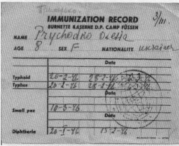

48

In June 1946, we had to leave that camp as it was being dissolved by the American Military Government and we were moved to the Mittenwald Refugee Camp which was also located in the Alps of Germany under the American Zone. The Mittenwald camp was made ready for us, the displaced people without a country. It was used for homeless people right after the Italian prisoners of war vacated the premises and returned to their native land of Italy. Although other nationalities settled in this camp, such as Poles, Latvians, Estonians, Lithuanians, Hungarians, and Russians, the biggest group was more than 2,000 Ukrainians. This majority group of Ukrainians began organizing cultural and education works. First they elected a Ukrainian Campus Council and then a Campus Administration Chairman. Soon schools were established. Wooden boards were found to make tables and chairs for school children and later for adults as well. Many adults had to learn new skills, academic or technical, in order to prepare themselves for earning a salary while living in a foreign country. Some of them had no training because they were taken away at the age of 14 or 16 to compulsory work in Germany during the war and others had skills that could not be applied to the foreign systems. The camp also had other activities formed such as sports, the theatre, churches (both Ukrainian Catholic and Ukrainian Orthodox), music school, the library, camp's printing press and broadcasting station, youth organizations such as *Plast* (Scouts), and care facility for sick people, invalids, old persons, and orphans. I attended Grade 3, while my sister Halia was in Grade 5 and took piano lessons. Mom was active with various literary groups and even performed on stage in some plays. She was a member of the theatrical group under the direction of M. Berezenko. I personally remember enjoying local puppet shows that were put on for the children. My stepdad was involved with the Ukrainian refugee camp administration.

Our Mittenwald Refugee Camp in the Alps.

My Grade 3 class. I am third standing on the left in 1947.

My Grade 3 report card dated May 30, 1947.
Signed in Ukrainian, German & here in English.

Our family of four settled in the block (building) above the communal kitchen which allowed us the good fortune of having a tiny room with two single beds, all to ourselves. On one of the walls was a mural of flowers with English words, "How are you?" I did not understand what it meant but the colourful flowers made the room look pretty. In addition to enjoying the mural, we were finally experiencing some stability and comfort. I was happy to have a whole bed where my sister and I slept together and a second bed for mom and stepdad. We had something to eat every day and on Sundays my stepdad would make us a treat. It was a slice of white bread, buttered, and sprinkled with white sugar on top. Once a week we were also given a raw egg which I had to swallow and, of course, I didn't care for that at all. We had to poke a hole at each end and suck out that slimy stuff. I was told I had to swallow all of it because it was good protein for me. We had no stoves in the refugee camp for cooking so I obediently performed that awfully disgusting task.

The most wonderful thing that all the kids in the camp enjoyed was the arrival of American soldiers one day. They drove inside the camp in their army vehicles, throwing out candy and gum for us. We ran after them and picked everything off the ground. It was great eating those candies and chewing gum, although we had to learn not to swallow the gum. Other great things in the camp were the weddings. When the bride and groom came out of the church, people outside would throw a few candies on them, something like confetti, and we looked forward to those weddings, hoping to get some of that candy off the ground.

Christmas time in Mittenwald introduced me to a new experience. I had always believed in *Sviatyy Mykolay* (St. Nicholas) who came in the middle of the night on December 19th. He would put a present under my pillow when I was asleep and, in the morning, the present would always be there for me to discover. When December 19th came around, I accidently woke up from my sleep and saw my mom putting something under my pillow. I kept my eyes shut so she would think I was still asleep, and that's when I finally realized who Santa really was. That Christmas we also had a Christmas tree in our little room and it was decorated with many animal pictures that mom drew, cut out, and hung on the tree. The best part was having a few real candies wrapped in coloured papers hanging on the tree. Sometimes my sister and I would sneak around and steal a candy from inside the wrapper, making sure that the wrapper still looked like the candy was inside because we could never have enough sweets. In the evenings, we would light the little candles placed on the tree branches and we would sing lovely Ukrainian carols.

Mom's 1946 Christmas decoration.

Being a child, I was quite happy living in this beautiful corner of the Bavarian Alps. When school was out, we would go to the forest outside the camp and pick strawberries and mushrooms, but we had to watch out for snakes. I recall an incident during our strawberry picking when I saw a big patch of berries. I kept very quiet so I would have all the strawberries to myself. As I bent down to pick them, a large snake crawled out and I screamed running away, leaving the strawberries behind. I hated snakes and was very much afraid of them, although it still did not prevent me from going to the forest. Besides visiting the forest, my sister and I would also play in the fields beside the camp where lovely field flowers grew. There were many different flowers and we would pick them and make pretty wreaths to wear on our heads, arms, or legs. One thing I was always careful of was cows, when we were in those fields. I still hated cows with big horns which I experienced earlier in Ukraine. It was a good thing that the cows in Germany had big bells around their necks which gave off loud sounds so that one could hear them before seeing them. We also spent many moments when my sister and I would lie on the ground among the flowers and look up at the sky, especially when the sky had pretty clouds. We'd imagine all kinds of things created by the changing shapes of the moving clouds. We'd even make up stories and give names to the different clouds. Out of all the things we did, I mostly loved picking and drying wild flowers. I have saved some of them to this day in my scribbler of pressed flowers under the label, "Herbarium collected in Mittenwald 1947 by Olesia Prychodko."

Halia and me outside the camp in early 1947.

In the Mittenwald camp, being already nine years old, I began growing up and learning new things. One of the things was my introduction to Ukrainian embroidery. Mom was able to find a piece of white cloth and a number of different coloured threads from somewhere and was teaching me how to cross stitch. I loved the colourful thread and the beautiful results that could be produced. It took me a long time to finish a piece of embroidery but eventually I turned it into a small cushion cover. I used the cushion for many years and washed it often. I still have it. Another skill I acquired, which I enjoyed doing, was mending socks, German style. It kept me busy and I was lovingly fixing many holes in many socks.

My first embroidery.

Our camp in Mittenwald was said to be the best organized refugee camp in all of the American Area camps because of the accomplishment of the administration by the Ukrainian occupants who provided cultural life for the children and the adults alike. A copy of the publication entitled, "ABROAD 1947 – One year's work of the Camp of Ukrainian emigrants (DPs) at Mittenwald" describes the life in detail, both in English and in German. My mother brought the pamphlet with her to Canada and it is still with me. Inside the pamphlet there were pictures and an account of the community life including education, music, theatre, churches, sports, and industrial workshops for self-sufficiency. These workshops, all taking place inside the camp, included shoemaking and tailoring, ceramics, knitting, and embroidery. It was important for refugees to work and, as the pamphlet's article quotes on page 39:

...we do not wish to live from mercy-bread. We at last wish to live like human beings!

Some refugees also worked outside the camp for the American Army and for the German firms. With a stable life in the camp and an opportunity to earn some spending money beyond the camp handouts, we were able to go on outings outside the camp. I remember when a group of our friends decided to go outside the camp to visit a mountain called Zugspitze. There was supposed to be some kind of lift that would take us to the top. When I arrived at the base of that mountain and looked up, my first reaction was fear. The more I looked up, the more I was frightened. I became so terrified that I made a decision not to go up that scary thing and nobody would make me. After convincing my stepdad of my paranoia, I stayed at the bottom with my mother while my sister, my stepdad, and others all went to the top of the mountain.

Halia with little boy, stepdad in glasses and friends on Zugspitze.

In spite of the favourable conditions of the camp, everyone knew that life for displaced persons in the camps was temporary. Therefore, the news about resettlement was of great interest to all. It was obvious that return to our native country of Ukraine was impossible due to the existence of the same Soviet regime under which people suffered for many years, so immigration to other foreign countries that welcomed refugees became a possibility. A number of refugees began leaving for Australia, South America, Canada or the USA. We wanted Canada because we had heard that Canada would protect Ukrainian refugees from involuntary repatriation to the USSR and hoped to be able to settle there. We knew that Russians continued forcibly grabbing Ukrainian refugees and deserters to send them back to Soviet Ukraine. Yet, at the same time, Russian propaganda was spreading news to the outside world that all of their citizens in the Soviet Union had the best life and lived in harmony within their union of nations; something similar to the cooperation of different cultures in the United States of America.

Our hopes were becoming a reality when, in the spring of 1947, my stepfather began corresponding with a very nice Canadian/Ukrainian family about our possibility of moving to Canada. We were getting excited, except for the fact that my sister got very sick. She was taken to the building inside our camp which was called The Hospital and there had an appendix operation. After the operation, my sister came home and was very weak, having a pretty difficult time recovering. To make her feel better, she received a present that she always wanted. It was a dog. She named him Bomchick and he slept with her and me in our bed. Although I would also play with him, the dog seemed to know that he belonged to my sister and not to me.

Summer was over and we were notified that this Canadian/Ukrainian family in Canada would sponsor us and send an invitation for our emigration to Canada. We were all thrilled that this wonderful country would be ours by the middle of 1948. We finally began believing that it would be possible for us to truly live like normal people.

As the chilly fall in 1947 had not yet arrived, it was a lovely warm day in September where the school was having a beginning of term sports activities. Winners of running races and various games received awards in the form of special ribbons. My sister won a number of ribbons but soon felt very weak and tired. After spending a few hours at home and not getting better, she was taken to the hospital where a few months earlier she had her appendix removed. By evening of that same day she was dead. She was thirteen years old. I was ten.

We were all in shock. What happened? What happened was that the appendix operation a few months earlier had caused infection throughout her whole body due to the unclean hospital and unclean surgical facilities. It took a few months for the poison to spread and finally kill her. I cannot describe the pain and the suffering that took place for us. My mom went into a state of extreme withdrawal. A priest tried to comfort her in our tiny room by bringing a book on life after death. The book contained pictures and a lot of explanation about heaven and hell, pointing out the path my sister would be taking by being an angel in heaven.

My last photo with my sister Halia just before her death in September 1947.

I saw those pictures in the book and wondered why so few people walked the narrow path towards the top of the mountain into heaven, while a whole bunch of naked people bounced and jumped around in a huge fiery cave down below, labeled hell. The priest's comforting didn't help mom. It seemed that nothing and nobody could relieve my poor mother's pain. My stepdad was silent and appeared disengaged from all of us. Outside our window, our dog, Bomchick, sat and howled.

Halia in a coffin, September 21, 1947.

We began preparing for the funeral and mom wouldn't leave my sister's side. Halia was put into the coffin and mom stayed beside it, bending down to wipe the blood that was trickling out of Halia's left nostril. Halia's coffin was a wooden painted box lined with white cloth and had fresh flowers all around her. I noticed that one of her eyes was slightly open and it scared me because I thought she might want to come back as a spirit and take me with her. She was my sister who lived with me all my life but somehow she did not seem the same dead. Being dead, she scared me. It took many, many years before I could look at Halia's funeral pictures without being afraid.

When the church service was over and the coffin was carried out of the church, we walked through the camp, down the main street, and out of the camp to the cemetery. The cemetery was approximately ten kilometers away in the village of Mittenwald. Everyone marched that distance; priests, altar boys, *Plast*

(Ukrainian Scouts), almost all of the camp inhabitants. Halia was carried by *plastuny* (scouts) of which she was a member herself. Mom, stepfather, I, and others followed behind the coffin.

Funeral procession inside the camp.

Funeral procession inside the camp.

Funeral procession outside the camp; everyone leaving the camp through the front entrance.

Funeral procession on highway to Mittenwald cemetery.

Cemetery.

No one could believe that a day before Halia was winning sports medals and a day later she was dead. Everyone loved my sister and everyone was in shock. When we finally reached the cemetery and more prayers were said, the coffin was sealed and before it could be lowered into the ground, mom knelt down wrapping her arms around it and wept.

Mom didn't want the coffin lowered into the ground and looked as if she was ready to jump into the grave herself. I remember being very confused at the cemetery seeing my mother down on her knees and weeping. I kept thinking that mom must not love me if she wants to leave me to be with Halia instead. After the funeral we came home and for the next few days we were all mournful and depressed. We all cried. I felt very alone without my big sister in my life and finally realized how very dear she was to me. My mom would hold me in her arms and stay silent. Our dog, Halia's Bomchick, disappeared and we never saw him again.

Besides the fact that we were living as homeless people in a foreign country, the loss of our Halia created another change in our family. My poor mother, who had already lost her beloved first husband, then an infant son, and now a teenage daughter, was facing another difficult situation. Her relationship with her second husband, my stepdad, was not satisfactory and there were talks of their separation. Before my sister's death, there was no indication that mom would split our family by leaving her husband. At least I was not aware of any such warning signs. Maybe that old scary event of Mykola Prychodko skeleton appearing to her after their first secret meeting was an omen for their incompatibility. It seemed that mom believed it had some validity. Whatever the reason, with Halia gone now, mom felt that the time had come to get a divorce. She said,

"I know that I am not a healthy person but I am still capable to take care of one child on my own."

Actually, the decision to separate was mutual. A letter I found, written by my stepfather to my mother in 1948, confirmed this. Another interesting point he made in his letter was how he felt about me. This may have some proof why I, as a child, did not like him.

LETTER – To mom before departure to Canada.

Tamara,
...Neither one of us loves each other; a quiet, organized family life we cannot have; each of us (you realize yourself) does not know how to care for one another; together we have no children; Lesia, after having lost Halochka, I cannot love. I think you can understand the reason for this. I analyzed everything and became convinced that you really never loved me.

Even in the early days, you couldn't forget about your first husband.   No wonder you kept thinking so often about him and never of me….
                                    Greetings, Mykola

P.S.   I think there is no reason for us to be enemies.

      Personally, I was pleased to hear of my mom's decision to divorce my stepfather.   I did not like him and I did not like having him in our family, in spite of everything he tried to do by protecting us from the horrors of war and doing all the good things to make sure we were kept safe and alive. I felt that finally I would have my mother all to myself and would not need to be a polite daughter to my stepfather. I also felt that it was important for me to get my surname changed back and be called Popadenko again.   I was proud to have the name Popadenko because it belonged to my real daddy and I became determined to get rid of the Prychodko name as soon as possible. But changing the surname had to wait because we had already started the process of immigrating to Canada under the name of the Prychodko family. Today, I do not understand why a name change was so important to me as a child and truly believe it was unfortunate that stepdad Prychodko and I kept a distance between us to the end.   I realize now that he tried to provide for us as good a life as he possibly could do, under such dire circumstances. After all, wasn't he the person admired by everyone who knew him?   He was a courageous man who had lived through much torture and suffering.   He was an author of published books, some of which I possess.   He had a brilliant mind and, unfortunately, I deprived myself of the gift of knowing him after coming to Canada.

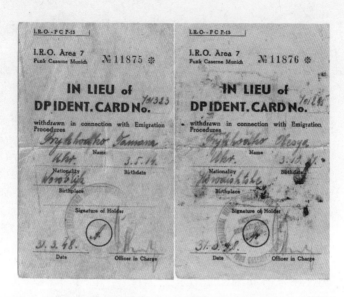

Mom's and my emigration cards dated March 3, 1948.

My official DP emigration picture. I am 10 years old.

When we finally left Mittenwald and arrived in Hamburg, we had to go through medical and dental services to get all our shots and be cleared of any physical problems. It was the first time I had ever been to the dentist and I was already ten years old. I had to sit down in a chair and look at all those scary drills. I was petrified. Seeing them, I kept my mouth shut and wondered how I could escape. At that exact moment, I actually jumped off the chair and ran out as fast as I could. I ran all the way outdoors and they never did get me back into that chair. So I never got my teeth checked and it wasn't until I turned sixteen years old that I had my first dental appointment in Canada. I do not remember ever brushing my teeth before coming to Canada. I do remember having loose baby teeth and, when they wouldn't fall out on their own, mom would tie a thread around the loose tooth with one end and the other end she would tie to a door knob. Then when the door knob was turned to open or shut the door, the string would pull the tooth out. Sometimes there would be blood and sometimes not.

We spent a fair amount of time in Hamburg and then, I believe, we went to Bremerhaven for our departure to Canada. I found a letter from one of mom's dear friends who lived with us in the same building in the Mittenwald camp, which said something about my mother. The letter was addressed to both mom and me, dated July 2, 1948.

Our dear Tamara and Dzyoun!
We already imagined that you are on the ocean, with waves carrying you to a new world. I even drew a picture for our little ones: Tamara stands on the ship, the wind blowing at her lovely black hair, in her eyes a mixture of sadness and hope. But you are still with us in Germany. I believe you will sail by July 6, so again

we wish you good voyage and good beginnings in the new life. Tamara, we were surprised when we heard what happened with you and Mykola. You are living apart? If this is truly final and serious, then I wish you, Tamara, strength, endurance, ability to find a place in your new life and nurture Lesia in it. You have to settle someplace among intelligent surroundings, use your knowledge of the Ukrainian language working as a pedagogue or in some publishing. Write me as soon as you arrive. Happy voyage! Lots of kisses to you and Lesia.

Vasyl, Nina and all occupants of room K62

The day finally arrived for us to get on the ship. July 5, 1948, the army ship named Beaverbrae was waiting for us. Originally the ship was used as an army carrier but after the war a lot of refugees got free passage on it to Canada. The voyage included three free simple meals per day. When we arrived at the dock, it was very early in the morning and the rain was pouring very heavily and hard. I saw the ocean for the very first time and I did not like what I was seeing. Everything appeared dangerous with the wind howling and the waves beating against the ship. With my previous fearful water experience, I thought,

What if we drown? The ocean looks so huge and deep with nothing in sight except water.

We got onboard and I was still pretty scared. And as it turned out, the ten day voyage was very turbulent and I did suffer from sea sickness during the entire trip. Whether my sickness was due to the strong waves and swells or whether it actually came from eating too many sweets is still debatable. For the first time ever, I saw sugar, jam, honey, all sitting on tables where we ate our meals. They were refilled when empty and never removed. It was a miracle. They were there all the time and left alone on all the tables without anyone guarding them at all. So, guess what happened? I began eating and eating, especially the jam. As I ate I could not believe my good fortune. That is when I decided, joyfully, that if this was an indication of what we would have in Canada, then I wanted Canada to be my home forever.

On the ship, the whole administrative process for overseeing refugee passengers was structured so that certain refugee men were assigned to look after certain duties.   One of these "in-charge" refugees was a particular Ukrainian man who drew attention to himself because of his strong belief in conveying to others that we must never stop trying to achieve Ukraine's independence, even living far away in distant places. He loved his native country and would not give up hope for its freedom from Soviet dictatorship. His name was Lewko Katola, although most people knew him as Lewko Moroz. He used the name, Moroz, as an alias to protect himself from the enemies who hated such patriotic Ukrainians as himself. He had to conceal his identity because of his activities in the Ukrainian Insurgent Army (UPA) fighting both the Nazis and the Soviets and later in his participation with the First Division of the Ukrainian Army on the German side. This man, Lewko, together with many other volunteers, became members of the Division not to aid the Germans but to protect their beloved Ukraine from Russia and fight the Russian Soviets. The Division of these Ukrainian soldiers was formed in the summer of 1943 when Hitler promised to liberate Ukraine from Soviet control. They joined the Division to try and stop the suffering, abuse, and starvation from Stalin's cruelty. They were also told that Hitler assured to ease the fighting on Ukraine's soil and would keep it from being completely destroyed. Unfortunately, Hitler's intention for his recruiting of Ukrainian soldiers was entirely selfish. He needed to gain more support against the Soviets because he was starting to lose the battle and wanted to use Ukrainians to increase his defense. This gave him an opportunity to send Ukrainian soldiers to battle ahead of his own so Ukrainians would be killed before the Germans. Hitler had no intention of freeing Ukraine and actually believed that the Ukrainian race was inferior to his Aryan superiority. He was willing to completely wipe out Ukrainians and did so by enslaving and murdering millions.

As our voyage continued, Lewko became friends with many different passengers and also met my mother. Mom and Lewko found much to discuss about their experiences during the war and agreed on many similar issues, one of them being their disappointment seeing the Soviet Union swallowing even more nations into their evil domination. At first Lewko explained to mom about his involvement with the Germans in the Division of Ukrainian soldiers where he completed all his training and became an officer. He told her how he survived all his battles and even his captivity in Italy. When they touched upon the topic of Ukrainian partisans and UPA, mom was surprised that Lewko had met mom's brother, Anton. Lewko said he admired her brother for being committed to saving Ukraine from destruction. As soon as mom found out that Lewko knew her brother, she wanted to ask all kinds of questions. She wanted to know how her brother was killed. Uncle Anton was tragically shot dead by the Russians in the forest and mom never recovered from grieving for him. She actually wrote a poem in his memory and later the poem was published. A bit of it, poorly translated by me, started something like this.

POEM – For my brother

There are no tears, my soul has turned to stone,
There are no words to express my sorrow,
I cannot believe that you are in the grave,
I cannot exist for my heart is filled with grief....

My uncle, mom's beloved brother, Anton, in 1942.

Mom wanted to learn more about her brother's death and continued searching for any additional information. I found a letter among mom's things which was addressed to her in early 1949. It went like this.

Tamara! Allow me to explain the matter of your brother. Maybe I'm writing about the wrong person, but I believe that your brother was this man. Year 1943, forest Bransk – I had an opportunity to meet with Anton of the partisan movement. At that time he was destroying railroads and trains with ammunition and enemy soldiers. Then when Russian partisans joined against the Germans, he left that area with his group and moved further west. I heard he

71

died in battle. Who killed him is difficult to say. War is war. Much happens in it. Forgive me, Tamara, but I cannot give you any more information. Maybe the person I'm writing about is not your brother. Please do not worry yourself. Only God knows the truth and people only guess about it. When we meet, we will talk more.

Greetings to you and thanks for your heartfelt friendship, M.

Unfortunately, I cannot decipher the signature of this person. But, I can still remember our escape with my uncle Anton's tank in the Carpathian Mountains.

During our whole voyage across the Atlantic, mom and Lewko met often to discuss things about the war, about my uncle, and about the hopes of someday seeing Ukraine become free. That's when I made up my mind that when I grew up, I would become an officer myself and go to war to fight for Ukraine's independence. I would become one of those people who transmitted secret messages and knew everything that went on around them. I would wear a uniform and everyone would respect me for my brilliance.

Lewko's interest in my mom increased even more after he learned that she was a teacher. Being an officer in battle, he had written many manuscripts about combat strategies and specific attacks on the enemy. He asked mom if she would look over a certain manuscript and correct any grammar mistakes that she found. Mom agreed to read his manuscript. This promoted more mutual interest and they seemed to be spending a great deal of time together. Although my stepfather Prychodko was on the ship with mom and me, he did not spent any time with us and was always involved with other people. The person who was spending too much time with my mother was this new friend of hers, Lewko. For that reason I did not like him. I felt he was taking my mom away from me and I wished that, when our voyage was finished, this man would go away and I would never have to compete with him for my mother's attention. I wanted mom all to myself and looked forward to having my wish come true when we arrived in Canada.

Lewko far right, stepdad Prychodko (no hat) and their new refugee friends on our ship in July 1948.

CHAPTER IV

Growing up in Canada

After ten long and turbulent days of sailing across the Atlantic Ocean, we finally reached Canada on July 15, 1948. I remember going down the Gulf of St. Lawrence and everyone commenting about it being the famous Canadian waterway. Once off the ship, we boarded a train for Toronto where many people got off, but we remained on the train to travel further west to Edmonton, Alberta. At the Edmonton train station, we were met by a person from the town of Westlock who sponsored us to come to Canada. He took us to his farm where we were greeted by many pleasant people. After a short rest in a private room, we were asked to join them for dinner. When dinner was served, I saw all those people sitting around a big table with tons of food on it and I couldn't take my eyes off the food. We were offered to eat everything and as much as we wanted. Everything tasted very delicious. As soon as we finished eating, I saw everyone dig into a little container and pull out tiny pieces of wood. They stuck the wooden pieces between their teeth. Then someone belched and apologized. I was surprised. How could people behave like this at the dinner table? Today, I have a completely different view of toothpicks and burping.

After a good rest and a great meal, we thanked the lovely people for their kindness of giving us a chance to come to Canada even though they knew all along that we would not stay on their farm. We returned to Edmonton where mom was getting a job teaching in a Ukrainian community school at the St. John's Ukrainian Orthodox Church. My stepdad was no longer with us and had his own plans for moving to Toronto.

With mom and me alone together, we looked forward to a new life in Canada that would be comfortable away from hardships and insecurities. We imagined this country having everything one would desire. My craving for sweets could certainly be satisfied by things like jam, candy, and ice cream. Mom and I moved into a small two-room attic of a house on 106 Avenue between 96 and 97 Streets. We shared the bathroom with an old lady who rented a room in the attic as well. The landlady downstairs allowed us to have a bath once per week, on Saturdays only, and would check the amount of water we put in the tub. She would say,

"Once a week, on Saturdays only, and just enough water to cover the depth of no more than five fingers. See here, insert your hand sideways by placing the little finger on the bottom of the tub and letting the water fill up to the touch of the thumb."

She was determined to control the use of water because she paid the utility bills. That tiny bathroom also kept my mother's pail of cold water. Every month she rinsed her sanitary rags in the toilet, soaked them in the pail, and then hung them to dry to be used the following month.

Summer of 1948 was wonderful. I had my mom all to myself and I loved it. We spent a great deal of time together and I enjoyed the fact that we could eat potatoes every day. We fried them, we boiled them, we baked them. September came along and I had to be registered in school in Grade one because I didn't know a word of English and I had just turned eleven years old. I made my mother sign me in as Lesia Popadenko instead of Olesia Prychodko because I wanted to get my real daddy's name back. Mom also changed her name and began signing it as Tamara Baranowska-Popadenko.

The worst thing that happened to me in the school was that I could not use my name, Lesia, because the teachers said it did not exist in the English language. They told me I had to be named Elsie, since it was as close to Lesia as I could have. I did not like Elsie and remember reading about it in class. I kept thinking,

Wasn't Elsie a cow in the pasture we read about in school? Why do people want to call me a cow? I am not going to keep the name Elsie and that's final.

Unfortunately, I did keep that name for the whole year. But outside the school, I was still called Lesia.

My mother and I were experiencing a wonderful, peaceful existence in this new country. We had food, a warm place to sleep and began meeting interesting people among the communities of Ukrainian pioneers and new refugees. I loved the feeling of complete fulfillment and satisfaction, having my mother always with me and expecting no perceived dangers or lack of food. With all the good things in our lives, something occurred in the late fall that I did not expect. The man from our ship, Lewko Katola (Moroz), decided to write to my mother. In his letter, he wrote about his proposal of marriage to her, saying he could not stop thinking about her. Mother was surprised and responded by writing back, emphasizing the fact that she was four years older than him, had been married twice, was not well, and had a young daughter. It seemed that her reply did not detract him from his desires because, in no time at all, he had arrived in Edmonton from Saskatchewan where he was living with relatives. I vividly recall his first appearance at the front door of our house. The doorbell rang and the landlady yelled for one of us to answer it. I ran down from the attic, opened the door, looked at him, and ran right back upstairs to mom. I recognized him and left him standing downstairs saying to mom,

"Mom, the white devil is here to see you."

I called him that because he had blond, balding hair, and I remembered him spending too much time with my mom on the ship. Mom went downstairs to meet him and asked me to go outside and play. When I returned, Lewko was gone and mom said that he had to go back to the farm in Saskatchewan where he lived with his relatives. Whatever transpired between the two of them was no longer important to me because he was not there and I hoped that he would stay away forever. Fortunately, he had left us; unfortunately, his letters kept coming. I found one of mom's letters where she responded to one of Lewko's letters.

Dear Lewko!
We are now facing a decisive moment in our personal lives. If your feelings towards me are those of a good friend, then my answer to marriage is no, but, if they are geared towards love of a woman, then I agree to becoming your wife. Consider also our Lesia. Even my good friends have cautioned you about children.

Tamara

My big surprise came in the spring of 1949 when Lewko showed up again and this time mom told me that she was going to marry him.

Lewko moved in with us into the two-room attic place and, once again, I lost my mom. He bought me a single bed to sleep on and mom slept on the old bed with him. The door between the two rooms became closed during the night and I found myself alone in bed and in a separate room. Although I didn't know Lewko at all, I still did not want him taking my mom away from me like other men did. She finally became all mine and I could have her all to myself. We had slept together in one bed, and during the day I would go to school but after school we were always together. Now with a new husband, she would turn her attention to him and I would not be important to her anymore. I so wanted to be important and loved. I wanted to be loved by my mother the way she loved me when there were just the two of us and the way I remembered being loved by my real daddy. Such an enormous need for affection existed in me most of the time. I hated sharing my mom with Lewko who appeared to be interested only in her and not in me. However, at the same time, I also realized that my life became more comfortable with his presence in it. He made sure that we had more food, better furniture in the house, and that my mom stopped working. I was able to join *Plast* (Scouting of Ukrainian Youth of Edmonton), and began forming new friends with young Ukrainian immigrants like myself. Those young sentiments of mine I found in a letter mom wrote to a friend in New York on August 27, 1949. This letter was sealed, addressed, stamped, but never mailed. Some of it she wrote,

79

My Lesia is now a real young lady. She goes to Plast – very grown up. But Halochka is gone.... Oh, Natalia, I suffer without her. My Lewko left for one month for harvest. I miss him very much. I don't work anymore and now have a gastrostaxis - buring of intestines - stomach sickness, a disease that's new to me and never had before. I am not complaining. We need to survive and believe that we will return to our beloved Ukraine.

Your Tamara

I am a Ukrainian Girl Scout (Plastunka) in 1949.

Mom loved her native Ukraine and everything to do with its culture and language. Mom was a brilliant, beautiful person who had the capacity to find joy in living, even with all her suffering and sickness.

Shortly after mom married Lewko, his cousin, Bohdan Chrustz, arrived in Canada from a DP camp in Germany. He moved in with us and I immediately liked him. With all four of us living together, we were becoming a nice, new family.

Mom dressed in Ukrainian costume in 1947.

Summer holidays were coming to an end and I was expecting to go to Grade four. This decision was based on my Grade three report card from the camp in Germany and on my limited knowledge of the English language.

I shall always remember the morning of August 29, 1949. Mom left the house to go to the store to buy some groceries. Lewko was still on the farm in Saskatchewan helping with harvest. Bohdan was at work at a printing press in Edmonton, and I was home alone waiting for mom to return from the store. I waited and waited and could not understand mom's long absence. Later that day, Mrs. Murynka, mom's friend, came to say that mom was at the Alexandra Hospital because she collapsed at the store and an ambulance picked her up. That evening I slept at Mrs. Murynka's place but before going to bed I prayed for a very long time to make sure that mom would get better and come back home soon. I usually always prayed at night before bed and, if occasionally I was too lazy to pray, I definitely would always cross myself before crawling into bed because that did not take much effort and I didn't have to kneel down. On this particular night, I prayed long and hard. I wanted God to make sure my mother was well again so that she would remain with me and not be taken away like my dad, my sister, and my baby brother. As I focused all my energy into praying for her health, I was not aware that my mom had already died.

The next day I came home and found both Lewko and Bohdan sitting on the bed. They were in tears as they told me that my mom died after having the whole left side of her body paralyzed. I sat beside them and my thoughts turned to God. Why did he take my mother away from me? Could it have been that I was a bad daughter when I would not listen to mom? Last winter she would make me wear those long heavy woolen underwear during cold weather and I would refuse putting them on. Or maybe I was too selfish in depriving her of happiness with my two stepfathers? There were times when I was jealous of their closeness to mom. Could this be part of the reason that contributed to her death? I asked God,

"God, please forgive me. I do not want my mom to die. I love her. I love her with all my heart and I want her back."

With mom gone, I wondered what would happen to me now? Where would I go? Who would protect me from danger? Oh, I should have been nicer to this man, Lewko. Would he keep me? He sat on the bed crying like a baby, after rushing home from the farm. I looked at him and immediately hoped he would want me to stay with him. But what if he does not? Would I be given to someone else? Who would want me? I have no one else. I realized that I had become an orphan with no relative in the entire world and I had just turned twelve years old.

Mom's funeral was held at our Ukrainian Greek Orthodox Church on 96 Street and 106 Avenue. Her body was lying in an open coffin. She looked very young and very beautiful, being only in her early thirties. That's when I thought to myself that I also wanted to die by age thirty so I looked as beautiful as my mother and everyone would feel sorry for me.

As I stood looking at her, someone gave me a lit candle on a long wooden holder and made me move closer to the coffin. I was told to bend towards my mom and kiss her good-bye. I would not do it because I was too afraid. I did not want to kiss or touch her. I heard people whispering how terrible I was not to kiss my own mother. After all, it was our custom for everyone to view the body before the coffin was closed and for some even to kiss the body. But I would not kiss mom and I wanted to run away. Although she did look beautiful, she also appeared like some strange cold creature. To me this corps was not my real mother. It was not the warm, soft, smiling mother I knew. It was some dead body that looked like my mother. I thought that if I touched her, she would pull me into the coffin and I would be buried alive together with her. I was very confused about death and very scared of dead people. I also did not know what happened to the soul of the dead person and that frightened me even more. I wondered if mom's spirit would hang around me all the time or where it would go now that she died. I was taught to believe that the spirit left the body at death and stayed on earth for forty days before going on to heaven for good. I knew this because our churches celebrated the passing of the soul into eternity forty days after death. A special day was arranged to go to church where people prayed and later had a big dinner where they mingled and said their farewells in honour of the person who had died forty days earlier.

As I moved further away from the coffin, I saw some women look at me disapprovingly, wondering why a daughter would desire to remove herself from the last opportunity of having the final presence with her departing mother. I closed my eyes and heard the choir singing *Vichnaya Pamyat* - a song which signifies the end of earthly existence and a wish for eternal peace to the deceased. Slowly the coffin was closed and carried out of the church with all of us following to the cemetery.

MRS. TAMARA KATOLA

ON Friday, August 31, Mrs. Tamara Katola passed away in the city at the age of 32 years. She is survived by her loving husband Mr. Leo Katola of Edmonton, 1 daughter Elsie Popadenko of Edmonton. A prayer service will be held on Saturday September 3, at 2:00 p.m. at the Chapel on the Boulevard.

Funeral services will be held on Saturday September 3, at 3:00 p.m. at the St. John's Ukrainian Orthodox Church. Rev. A. Chrustawka will officiate and interment will take place in the Edmonton Cemetery.— Park Memorial Limited, Funeral Administrators and Directors; (The Chapel on the Boulevard).

Mom's obituary and my name Elsie.

Cemetery: Lewko and Bohdan on the right; friend Lillian on the left, September 3, 1949.

At the cemetery, mom's coffin was put into the ground and, as we all threw bits of dirt into the grave, I wondered what would happen to me now. Within days, two English speaking people came from the Government Child Welfare Department and started asking me questions through an English/Ukrainian interpreter. They asked if I would like to move in with a nice family and live with them permanently. I panicked.

What should I do?

At this point, I did not want to be taken away from Lewko and Bohdan. I felt that I should trust these two men because they knew my mother and my mother trusted them. We all came from similar Ukrainian war-time experiences and I would be able to relate to them, even though Lewko's marriage to mom lasted less than six months. To go live with strangers would be worse than with someone who had loved my mother. So, I quickly said I would like to stay with Lewko if he wanted me and he was surprised that I was assuming otherwise. He told me never to worry again because he was committed to raising me as his daughter and he would take good care of me. We then both informed the English man and woman, again through an interpreter, that I wanted to remain with Lewko and have him as my guardian.

Now that it was confirmed that I would live with Lewko and Bohdan, the three of us moved to another building where many Ukrainian immigrants stayed. We had one room with me sleeping on the little bed and Lewko and Bohdan sleeping on the sofa that opened up into a double bed. We had to go down the hall to use the sink, the bathtub, and the toilet. These three things were inside a room, each separated by walls of vertical boards that did not quite reach the ceiling. Everyone who lived on that floor had to use them. Inside that room something interesting happened to me one day that I did not know before. I was sitting on the toilet and heard someone taking a bath next to me. I noticed a hole in the boards and peaked through it. What I saw was pretty scary for me. A man was getting out of the tub and turned towards me. He was hairy and his private parts were right at my face. I had never seen a naked man before and quickly ran out of there afraid to tell anyone about it.

All my worries about my future life soon disappeared because of my new stepdad Lewko. He told everyone that he was going to raise me as the perfect, intelligent, caring individual in honour of my biological parents in heaven. He even researched a much better school for me and made arrangements through the Ukrainian nuns of St. Josaphat's Church that I attend Sacred Heart School. My new school turned out to be wonderful because I was put into grade six, after being tested by the teacher-nuns, and was allowed to keep my name Lesia. I loved having nuns for my teachers because they created a peaceful atmosphere and I wondered if maybe I should become a nun myself and live with them in the convent.

Because Lewko's faith was Ukrainian Greek Catholic, the majority faith of Western Ukraine, and my mom and I had Ukrainian Greek Orthodox faith, the majority in Eastern Ukraine, I changed going to church from Orthodox to Catholic. I started going to confession and communion in the Ukrainian Catholic Church and found little difference between the two churches, other than the fact that in the Orthodox Church I did not need to tell my sins aloud to the priest during the confession whereas I had to do so in the Catholic Church. The word "Greek" appeared with both Ukrainian Orthodox and Ukrainian Catholic because Ukraine's Christianity originated from the Byzantine Empire, at Constantinopol, Greece in the year 988. For Ukraine, there were many struggles between the Orthodox and the Catholic faiths, mostly due to the country's political divisions which came from foreign invaders occupying Ukraine.

At home, Lewko was determined to be a great stepfather, who I called Lewko. He always expected nothing less than perfection from me. My school grades could not be less than a B (A being top honours). My activities outside school had to be approved by him and he had to always know exactly where I was and what I was doing. I had to keep my hair in braids and wear the type of clothes he permitted. I had to be very punctual with curfew, coming and going out of the house on time. I remember, at the age of thirteen, coming home about ten minutes late after caroling one Christmas evening. When he opened the door, he glanced at me, and said,

"Yes, what is it you want? I'm sorry, I don't know who you are. My daughter does not come home late."

He slammed the door shut and I stood outside shivering in the cold and crying. He made me wait at the door for a short while and then he let me in, emphasizing the fact that I was never to be late again. Stepdad Lewko was very strict and allowed me absolutely no freedom. He was an army officer during the war and treated me like one of his soldiers. I do remember the times being caught disobeying him which had resulted in physical punishment. During such disciplinary moments, I was glad to have Bohdan with us for moral support but, sadly, it did not last long because he had tuberculosis and quickly left Edmonton for treatment at the sanatorium in Prince Albert, Saskatchewan.

So now I was left with no protection from my domineering stepfather Lewko, whose disciplinary parenting controlled every aspect of my young life. Because I also knew he wanted the best for me, I tried not to disappoint him. He bought me nice clothes and created a safe, comfortable environment in which to live. What I mostly enjoyed living with Lewko was our love of music. We both wanted music in our lives and devoted much time to singing in different choirs and in private on our own. Lewko played many instruments and had a guitar, so he would teach me to play the guitar. On Sundays, after church, we would have singing and guitar playing sessions together at home. I took piano and singing lessons, violin and dancing lessons. Because I could not hold the violin properly under my chin and was unable to stand on toes in ballerina slippers, I did not have to continue with the last two.

Lewko and me playing guitars and singing in 1951.

Lewko and I lived in a very structured environment where I followed his rules for over two years. Then he decided he would marry again. It was interesting when he brought different women to the house and later would ask me what I thought of them. I actually did not like any of them until the time he brought home an attractive woman called Olga Pinkowski. She was a Canadian/Ukrainian woman with beautiful clothes, lovely curled hair, and wore great hats. She was born in Canada and could speak both English and Ukrainian fluently. Our community knew her as the famous soprano singer whose nickname was Pinkie. Of course, I approved of their marriage and, of course, I would love to have her for my stepmother. In no time, the wedding was set. Three days before it, I had my hair washed and put in ringlets to be ready for the special occasion. When the wedding date arrived, I was adorned with a new dress, silver shoes, my hair in ringlets, and I felt like a princess. I was fourteen and a half years old.

Wedding: I am with Lewko and Pinkie in 1952.

I realized that there would be some changes in my life and looked forward to a new relationship with this attractive woman. Unfortunately, we had a difficult time getting to know one another. It all started a few days after their wedding. Lewko suggested we all go to the movies to celebrate our new family. Pinkie got upset and said,

"Lesia can't come with us. This is our honeymoon."

"Fine, if you don't want anything to do with her, I will take sole responsibility for raising Lesia. When we have our own child, you can take care of it and I will take care of Lesia." Lewko replied.

And that was our beginning. A relationship that was not so great for either of us. By the way, I did not go to the movies that day. Later came the rule about "No Meat on Fridays." It was a sin to eat meat on Fridays because the Pope of the Catholic Church said so. Pinkie was a devout Catholic and made sure no one touched any bits of meat on Fridays. Once I ate a piece of *kovbasa* (garlic sausage) on a Friday which resulted in a huge argument. Pinkie would be very angry and Lewko would say,

"Leave the kid alone. She's gone through starvation and war, let her have some meat."

We continued having disagreements until Pinkie gave birth to a baby boy, Orest, who we called Joujee. My love for this sweet little boy made us somewhat closer.

Little Orest and me in 1957.

91

I was thrilled when, on my sixteenth birthday, Pinkie offered to take me to have my long braids professionally cut off at a beauty parlour. I was very thankful to her because I waited for that moment for a very long time. I knew Lewko did not want my braids cut off and worried about the outcome. Lewko was furious at first but eventually he was all right with my new short hair style and it did not ruin my relationship with him.

Pinkie and I got friendlier, although I never felt any maternal nurturing from her. I was glad I could continue relying on Lewko for guidance and support. I also knew he was a very busy person with many commitments. He had a physically demanding job loading railway ties into boxcars; he played soccer on Ukrainian teams; he sang in different choirs; he typed many letters on a Ukrainian typewriter which he sent to his family in Western Ukraine and to other Ukrainian nationalists who were also hoping to save Ukraine from the Soviet destruction. In Canada, Lewko was still experiencing homesickness with the strong desire for Ukraine's independence from Russian domination. I even heard that he was an informant with the RCMP on Communist activities but I had no proof and knew nothing about the Cold War that was still among us. Lewko did not speak English and hoped to return to his native country of Ukraine. Actually, my entire life was also totally Ukrainian except for the fact that I was attending school during the day where I spoke English. Other than that, I spoke only Ukrainian and interacted with Ukrainian people where I belonged to Ukrainian

Scouts (*Plast*) and to Ukrainian choirs. Later, when I turned twenty years old, I took several Ukrainian history courses at St. John's Institute. I sang in a Ukrainian quartet which was created and conducted by Maria Dytyniak. The following year, at age twenty-one, I began announcing the weekly Ukrainian Program on the radio under the direction of Mr. K. Telychko.

My participation in *Plast* (Scouts) gave me a healthy feeling of friendship among its members. This organization had its roots from England's Baden Powell taking on a Ukrainian flavor a few years later in Western Ukraine which lasted to 1930. After World War II, *Plast* resurrected its existence in refugee camps in Germany and Austria. My sister was a member but I was too young then. I joined later in Edmonton where I was able to form many good friendships there. We met for our weekly meetings at a permanent place (*domivka*) in the basement of St. Josaphat's Church on 97 Street. Besides learning to be good, caring Canadian citizens, we continued acquiring knowledge about the history and arts of our native Ukraine. I loved going to *Plast* meetings and especially loved attending summer camps which were held at SeeBa Beach Lake, south of Edmonton. *Plast* members also took part in many special celebrations. For example, I recall Canadian Prime Minister Louis St. Laurent coming to Alberta in 1953. We, members of *Plast,* formed a human chain for him to pass. *Plast* continues its existence to this day and, in September 2008, celebrated its successful Sixtieth Anniversary in Edmonton.

Ukrainian Guides and Scouts in 1953; I am third on the right.

QUARTET HONORS LEADER—A concert honoring Col. Euhen Konovalets, late leader of the Ukrainian liberation movement, will be held at 8 p.m. Sunday in Alberta College auditorium. Featured vocalists will be the above quartet, consisting of, left, to right, Zirka Klymkovych, Lesia Popadenko, Luba Strangret, Mariyka Tatchyn.

Our quartet's concert performance in 1959; I am far right.

I was becoming a competent young woman, having graduated Grade 12, but was never allowed to date unless Lewko approved the boy who could only be a Ukrainian and a university graduate or a university student. I was also reminded that I was to remain a perfect candidate for becoming a wife and to keep myself pure and mysterious. Lewko would say,

"There are two kinds of woman: those that men want to marry and those they don't. The expression, 'Why buy a cow if you can get milk for free,' means that once a woman is "shop soiled", she becomes second hand merchandise and no man wants to marry her."

I listened to Lewko's guidance and remained that perfect person for all to admire until I became a married woman. Unfortunately, this did not result in a romance or in a promising boyfriend for me. During my melancholy days, I would turn to that old imaginary world I had created during the war where the ugly light bulb became a beautiful doll. I would imagine being in a place where all my desires and hopes were fulfilled. Sometimes I would write how I was feeling. My first musing began,

What is the benefit of life itself? Can it be warmth and human understanding? Or is it hatred and corruption pending?

Although I was fully aware of surviving my past struggles and now lived with a kind, good family, I still continued missing my mom and my dad. Thinking of mom, I decided that it was important for me to take better care of her grave and plant some fresh flowers. So I planted lots of bedding plants and would take the bus twice a week to water them. One time when I got to the cemetery, I could not find the watering can that used to sit next to the outdoor water tap. I looked everywhere and finally decided to go into the stone building that held cremated bodies inside. Although I felt uncomfortable, I opened the heavy door and slowly walked in, noticing the water can. As I let go of the door to reach for the can, the door slammed shut with a loud bang. I grabbed the can and went for the door. The door would not open. My heart stopped beating. I said aloud,

"Oh, God, please get me out of here! I am so scared being surrounded by all these dead beings."

Then I remembered my guardian angel and found my inner strength. I became aware of all the pretty flowers surrounding me and noticed the sun's rays peeking through a stained glass window high above. I tried to control my fear and a story I once heard from Bohdan, Lewko's cousin, came to mind. He told me about his experience during the war in Germany when he was running away from the Nazi soldiers. He said he was able to find a safe place in the cemetery. Because cemeteries in Germany had small buildings where bodies were kept in coffins before their burial, Bohdan was able to crawl under a body and hide himself. I could not imagine lying under a corps and convinced myself that my situation was nothing like his. I calmed down and tried the door again, turning the handle with all my strength. The door opened and I ran out, thanking my angel as well.

During my high school years, I had worked part time at the Army & Navy Store on 97 Street because we had little money to live on, especially with Lewko trying to send as much as possible to his family in Ukraine. Right after graduation, instead of going to study at university, where I was offered an opportunity to take the Ukrainian Studies program at the University of Alberta, I rejected the offer and got a job as a secretary in the Department of Education with the Provincial Government. I had excellent typing and shorthand skills because I took Business courses as options in high school. I gave half my salary to Pinkie and the rest was all mine. First thing I bought was a portable sewing machine and began making my own clothes. I loved to sew, to embroider, to sing, and to eat. Although I was already twenty-one years old, I continued living under Lewko's control, focusing on his ideas of what was important in my life. I was insecure without his feedback and could not jeopardize the safety I felt with him. This need for his approval created a dependency where I believed he was my only protector in the whole world, which was actually quite true. Over the years, I learned to behave the way he expected me to behave without really getting to know myself to discover what I needed and wanted in life. Such conditioning made me take this safer path, which prevented me from exploring my own distinct thoughts, actions, and desires. I continued feeling some resentment as well as some fear towards Lewko and would often find myself escaping into my own imaginary world. Secretly, I never stopped hoping and daydreaming that one day I would find a husband with whom I would live happily for the rest of my life. It seemed I was looking for a fairytale romance with a Prince Charming. I had created all kinds of fantasies for myself, knew the Cinderella and Snow White stories and hoped to be rescued by a prince. And so I waited.

CHAPTER V

Marriage and children

June 4, 1960, at twenty-two years of age, I married Michael Hawrelak. Michael was a university student, a Canadian/Ukrainian who could speak Ukrainian, and had a distant relative, Bill Hawrelak, who was the mayor of Edmonton. Michael was a perfect husband for me, approved by my stepfather, Lewko. I also liked Michael and was excited to begin a new life away from Lewko's constant control. Michael was very handsome, had a car, was a great cook and gardener, and opened a world for me I had never known before. A world where everyone could enjoy a life of freedom and fun, have an opportunity to fulfill their own desires, and become pleased with their own lifestyles. Initially, that type of mentality made me feel alienated because I grew up basically on the notion that in life "one suffers and eventually one dies." But now, I tried to see the possibility of getting the same satisfaction of leading an exciting, unrestricted life, in spite of the fact that I was very much aware of the many differences that existed between my own growing-up experiences and those of my husband.

Michael married me, but he did not know the real me. He knew the pretty, likeable individual who could be lots of fun and who enjoyed his company. I do not think I really knew or truly understood Michael either. I felt very fortunate to have him for my husband and future father to my children. My intentions for being a good wife were to become a domestic tycoon where I would take care of my husband's needs, maintain all household and family responsibilities, contribute to Ukrainian culture and church activities, and become a martyr if necessary. I would be the catalyst for the wellbeing of our family and would respect my husband as the head of the family. This is what was expected of a good, traditional Ukrainian woman and I was going to be all that and more.

Thank you ever so much for your lovely gift!

Lesia and Michael
June 4th 1960

My wedding, Michael and me, June 4, 1960.

To begin our married life, Michael and I moved to Calgary where he enrolled in the Education Faculty at the University of Calgary and I got a job there as a secretary at its new campus. After eleven months of marriage, I was blessed to have my own daughter to shower her with my affection. In honour of my love for my mother, I chose to name my daughter Tamara (Tammy for short). The baby began to fill the void that I had been yearning for all my life. This unconditional love shared in a bond between mother and child is richer than any I had experienced. To further my maternal love, four years later, my second daughter arrived. We named her Katherine (Kathy). Becoming a mother and having my daughters in my life was the most precious, wonderful feeling of bonding and love. I devoted my full attention to raising them and marveled at the abundance and attachment a mother has in reserve to be showered on her children.

After five active years of marriage, Michael graduated and started teaching. I quit working and was glad to stay home with the children. Besides being a proud mother, I was active in my Ukrainian community and spent a great deal of time where I sang in the choir, belonged to St. Vladimir's Ladies' Aid Society, contributed to the Ukrainian school, dancing, concerts, and provided much assistance with catering for bazaars and dinners. I was pleased with my life, but there was one more thing I wanted to do. I wanted to start taking university courses in the evenings on a part time basis to learn things at a higher, formal level. Maybe my reasoning stemmed from an early age with my parents stressing the fact that learning was important or maybe the expression "ignorance is bliss" did not appeal to me. I was not interested in a career path as much as knowing about people, survival, life after death, beliefs, and everything associated with understanding human nature. I decided to major in Philosophy and realized the material I was learning encouraged my kind of thinking and increased my desire to find out what I really wanted out of life and how I could feel more secure. I also took Religious Studies courses searching for the knowledge of spiritual beliefs and whether life after death did exist. My fear of both the supernatural and death did not disappear from me and I wanted to know what other religions and science had for explanations. Although I was a Christian who went to church every Sunday and was taught the beliefs of the Catholic and the Orthodox faiths, I needed more knowledge to shed my fears.

Busy with all my commitments to everything I wanted to do, I was becoming more confident in trusting my own judgment. After twelve years of marriage, in late 1972, I was suffering from an acute inflammatory skin disease (erythema nodosum) and was being treated for it when I became surprisingly pregnant with my third child. I needed to weigh the risk of continuing the pregnancy due to the unsafe treatment and found it was worth it. My miracle baby girl arrived not only healthy, but who also cured me of my disorder. Although little Jennifer was not planned, she was "the apple of my eye." Now, we had three daughters and I was totally and completely connected to them, thrilled for having these precious little people in my life. Gradually, as time went by, I started questioning my marriage, realizing my aloofness towards my husband was creating a problem. It seemed that all my love and attention was spent on my children and I did not go out of my way to be that good, perfect, traditional Ukrainian wife I once wanted to be for my husband.

Something I appreciated being married to Michael was meeting his whole family. They were Ukrainian pioneers from Bukovina, Ukraine who introduced me to many stories about the hardships that existed for these early settlers. Michael's *baba* (grandma) talked about living inside one of those dugout earth dwellings underground (*burdey*) as a child, but by 1940 her house was considered for a Master Farm Award. (It is now located at the Ukrainian Cultural Heritage Village fifty kilometers east of Edmonton.) I also learned about the mistreatment of these early Ukrainian pioneers who worked hard to clear the forest of trees and stumps, eventually turning the land into the fertile soil we have today. Often these hard working men were called by a derogatory word *bohunk* which implied a dirty, illiterate drunk. I was explained how Canada accused these Ukrainian immigrants being Austrian enemies during World War I and how they were imprisoned into the internment camps. (Exhibit can be viewed at Banff's Cave and Basin, Alberta.) These immigrants were victims in their own country and the same injustice was happening to them in Canada. Either Canada did not realize that they came from Western Ukraine which was occupied by Austro-Hungarian Empire during that period or maybe Canada was getting somewhat worried that those Ukrainian/Canadians did not fit into its creation of the English Anglo-Saxon country. It was obvious to see that the Canadian landscape was beginning to change with the erection of Ukrainian churches and homesteads of houses with thatched roofs. For whatever reason, such discredit did take place but it happened many, many years ago and things did improve over time for their children. The second generation of those Ukrainian pioneers saw an opportunity to become sophisticated members of our society. For example, the 24th Governor-General of Canada, R.J. Hnatyshyn, was a son of one of those Ukrainian/Canadian pioneers. Even in my lifetime in Canada, I have seen many changes for the better. Now, in Edmonton, we have English-Ukrainian bilingual classes taught in the public school system. Concerning my name Lesia, I get favourable reactions to its uniqueness with no need to change it to my unhappy days of being named Elsie. It's also amazing that in pioneer days, sheepskin coats of Ukrainian immigrants were made fun of; today, these sheepskin coats have become a fashion statement.

Going back to my first Christmas holiday as a married woman during 1960-61, Michael and I travelled to Edmonton to be with Lewko and Pinkie. At the house, we were introduced to the visitor from the United States who was Lewko's close war buddy. Both men were Ukrainian partisans and later both served with the First Division of Ukrainian Soldiers on the German side in WWII to fight Russian Soviets on Ukrainian soil. Although they now lived in democratic countries of North America, their souls longed for their native Ukraine. The two seemed to be spending much time discussing past and future events of Ukraine and its people. Lewko never stopped hoping for an independent Ukraine and would do everything possible to achieve that goal. His visitor and friend, Liubomyr Ortynsky, had similar hopes for a free Ukraine, as did all the members of that Division who currently belonged to the "Brotherhood of Former Soldiers of the First Division of the Ukrainian National Army." This Brotherhood group was formed after the war in 1950 and its president, Dr. Ortynsky, was spending Christmas with us. I remember when Lewko and Dr. Ortynsky were talking about Ukraine's necessity to achieve independence and complete separation from Russian domination. This is something that always existed among Ukrainians; those living in Ukraine and those in the diaspora. Even Taras Shevchenko (1814-1861), a great Ukrainian poet and painter, had dreams to see Ukraine as an independent country without interference from foreign rulers, and especially Russia. He believed and claimed that his beloved Ukraine was not Russia and that the Ukrainian language was not the Russian language, in spite of being arrested and sent to Siberia for writing patriotic poetry.

Less than three months after Dr. Ortynsky's visit, on March 17, 1961, Lewko was killed at work, crushed by a pile of railway ties he was about to load into boxcars at the Canada Creosoting Company. Apparently, a number of ties toppled over and slid down the pile carrying him with them.

105

Dr. Ortynsky, me, Michael and Pinkie, Christmas 1960.

Shortly after Lewko's death, Dr. Ortynsky died July 22, 1961 in New York. Were their deaths a result of their zest for Ukraine's independence? We heard whispers that their deaths could be due to the Soviet murderous system. We were still living in Cold War times where KGB and other secret Soviet goonies around the world made sure people like Lewko and Dr. Ortynsky were silenced. I personally did not want to believe such talks, but then I wondered why Lewko used his alias, Moroz, if he truly felt safe from his enemies. Years later, Bohdan, Lewko's cousin, told me that immediately after Lewko's death, a burly looking Russian came to Prince Albert Sanatorium where he was being treated for TB and told him not to worry as nothing will happen to him like what had happened to his brother, Lewko.

Lewko's funeral took place at St. Josaphat's Ukrainian Catholic Cathedral on 97 Street. Seeing him lying in a coffin dressed in the Ukrainian white shirt that I sewed and embroidered for him, I looked at his face but would not touch any part of him or the coffin. I was still afraid of dead people, just as I was afraid of my sister and my mother years ago. Those early fears of the dead never left me and they always continued frightening me. With Lewko, it was even worse because he promised me that when he died, he would come back to me as a spirit and tell me all about the other world to which we enter after death. The fear of his spirit visiting me, especially during the night, remained with me for many years. Now, standing close to the open coffin, I tried to control my fear by barely glancing at his body and internally saying to myself,

Lewko, don't you dare show yourself to me now that you are dead.

After Lewko's death, my stepmother, Pinkie, and her eight year old son, Orest, came to live with me and Michael for approximately two years. Our relationship was always strained but we both tried to make it work. One thing that Pinkie and I did share was our love for little Orest. Later, they moved back to Edmonton to live with Pinkie's ailing mother. The sad thing was that eventually Pinkie was getting very sick herself and was spending her last days in the hospital. I kept in touch until her passing in 1989. At the funeral, I saw her lying in a coffin and got enough courage to put my hand on her folded hands and say good-bye. Her hands were very cold and, although my fear of the dead was slowly lessening, I have never touched another dead person since.

Orest and I are still in contact with one another. He lives in Edmonton, happily married to Irene (Irka) with his own lovely, grown family.

In the late 1970, I was fortunate to reconnect with Lewko's coursin, Bohdan, my old childhood step-uncle who lived with us when mom was still alive. His treatment at the Prince Albert Sanatorium cured him of TB and introduced him to Marge Johnson who worked there. A romance developed between them and later led to a happy, long marriage. Bohdan played a very special part in my life for he was my only link to my mother. He would tell me stories about my mother and how brilliant, pretty and talented she was. He would say that she loved me very much and often worried about her poor health. Those were always my most delightful conversations for they connected me to my special childhood memories. Every fall, Bohdan and Marge visited us and brought all kinds of fresh vegetables from their luxurious garden. Sadly for all of us, Bohdan passed away on June 4, 2006. Marge still lives in Prince Albert and we are fortunate to keep in touch with her.

When Lewko died, so did my total dependency on the only person who kept me safe and who told me how to behave and how to make the right decisions. For the next fourteen years after his death, I was trying to grow up and take complete responsibility for all of my actions. My husband was an easy going man who seldom opposed my views and said I was smart enough to figure things out on my own. With my daughters growing older, I began confiding in them, especially Tammy, my oldest, and decided I would be much happier if I let my husband go. I believed that he deserved a wife who would love him dearly, and I would finally get my complete freedom. I wanted such freedom to experience a life without any commitments to a husband or to any other man. I believed I was confident enough to raise my daughters as a single parent. They were good, smart, considerate, well behaved and beautiful children. So, in the summer of 1975, fifteen years after our wedding, Michael and I decided to separate and then got a divorce. At first I felt as if I had committed a crime and stopped going to church and to all those Ukrainian functions because I was ashamed to interact with the parishioners as a divorcee and also because I was too busy. I got a full time job working at the university and continued with part time courses toward my Philosophy degree. I also took courses in Business Management to secure a possible advancement in my university career.

As days went by, I became aware that my life with my daughters was peaceful and orderly. I was pleased with my accomplishments as a mother and I was proud to have them as my daughters. We were all very close and spent many intimate moments where we confided in each other, cared for each other, and learned from each other. Besides overseeing their school work and individual house responsibilities, I took the girls on Sunday picnics to Edworthy Park and in the summer we enjoyed many camping outings in the Rocky Mountains. I wanted to raise my daughters in an environment where they felt secure and loved, something I had missed in my own later childhood years. Although Michael was a good man, he did not connect with his daughters as closely as I did because they were girls and not boys. For me, it was crucial to make my daughters believe that they were the most important people in my life and that I would always be there to protect them from any unforeseen harm.

Being a mother myself now, I remembered and cherished my own mother's gentle singing to me before bedtime. So when my daughters were little, I too sang Ukrainian songs to them and talked about fairies and butterflies, the way she did with me. When my girls got older, I told them stories about the war and the tragic experiences I had lived through as a child. It was important to me that they knew what I had survived and how I came to live in Canada. I also wanted them to see how I loved my Ukrainian heritage and hoped to pass this on to them.

I made sure they were good students, took piano lessons, belonged to Girl Guides, had swimming lessons, and respected older people. As far as my divorce was concerned, it was amicable and I can honestly say that it did not create animosity nor destroy our respect for one another. Michael and I both wished each other a stress free life and successful achievement of happiness. As far as our girls were concerned, they had complete freedom to spend as much time with their dad as they desired, which resulted in their continued relationship with him.

I promised myself I would never marry again because I did not want a stepfather for my daughters, having had lived with two stepdads myself. In addition to taking care of my daughter's needs, house and yard duties, all finances, full time working, and part time studying, I did find the time to date a few interesting gentlemen from the university and others outside campus life.

In no time, I was celebrating my 50th birthday in 1987. I enjoyed my life of freedom and was delighted to see my daughters developing into beautiful, successful, young adults. Tammy had already graduated with a B.Sc. in Computer Science from the University of Calgary, Kathy had completed high school, and Jennifer was attending junior high school in the French immersion program. At work, I earned a number of promotions, making a better salary, and had good friendships that were formed on campus. I continued taking interesting courses towards my degree and even decided to pursue some sports, such as long distance running, windsurfing in the summer, and skiing in the winter. My girls and I were in good health, shared a happy, secure home, and I could not imagine wanting anything more in my life. Looking back on my struggle to survive during and after the war, it was hard to believe how wonderful my life has turned out.

My 50th birthday in 1987.

My daughters: Tammy, Jen, Kathy in 1985.

CHAPTER VI

Surprise Reunion

Eight months later, in the spring of 1988, the Mathematics Department at the University of Calgary had a visitor from Kyiv University of Ukraine through the Academy of Sciences Exchange Program. This professor wanted to meet a Canadian/Ukrainian to find out what a Ukrainian immigrant remembered of the old country. As soon as I was introduced to him, he was surprised that I was no different from him with the knowledge of the Ukrainian language, culture, music, and general history of Ukraine. What surprised me was that he told me about the new political situation taking place in the Soviet Union. He assured me that soon Ukraine would gain its independence. I did not believe him. It has been more than three-hundred and fifty years that our Ukraine was subjugated by foreign invaders. At first Ukraine was invaded by the Turks and Tatars, then Austrians, Poland and now Russia of the USSR, so how true could it be. A free Ukraine was something that every Ukrainian hoped for, for many, many years with no success. What I wanted to know from him was something about my father. Because my father had taught at the University of Kyiv and because this visitor was teaching there now, I wondered if he could find out when and how my father died. I told the visitor that I became an orphan as a child and had no

113

way of knowing what happened to my father. He took my information and said that when he returned to Kyiv, he would get his graduate students to do some research into getting information about my dad.

Shortly after his departure to Kyiv, I received a letter from this visiting professor. The letter, typed in Ukrainian words, came to my office. I opened it and started reading.

Dear Lesia!

I am happy to inform you that I was able to locate news about your father. Your father is alive and is living in Leningrad. His address …. His telephone….

Your friend, Wilhelm.

I froze in shock.

How could this be true? My daddy alive? My daddy who loved me as his precious little girl? My daddy who I always loved and missed all my life? This was insane!

But there it was; my dad's name, his address, and his telephone number. He had a wife but no children. He was living in Russia, in Leningrad (the city's name was changed back to St. Petersburg after the breakup of the Soviet Union in 1991). I stared at the letter and kept reading every word over and over. I picked up the phone and called my daughter, Tammy, at her work. To this day, she remembers my hysterical outburst. "He's alive! He's alive!" was all she heard. I temporarily lost the ability to speak English and was

114

talking in Ukrainian. Through tears, she began telling my story to a co-worker. By the end of the story, the entire office was full of people listening to the surreal events about her mother and grandfather.

I could not work for the rest of the day. I came home, sat motionlessly by the kitchen table and stared at the letter, repeatedly reading over each word. Outside, I heard noises from cars blowing their horns and approaching my house. The cars stopped and people came out yelling, "Lesia has a father!" It was a celebration for me, organized by my friend and co-worker, Bev Frangos, arriving with office staff and some graduate students of the Computer Science Department. They were carrying balloons, wine, snacks, and cheerful greetings to help me rejoice in my new discovery.

The next day, it was still difficult for me to settle down but I went to work. I had the letter with me and, after checking the time difference between Calgary and Leningrad, I decided to phone Russia. At the appropriate time, I dialed the number in the letter. The phone was ringing and my heart was pounding. Someone on the other end picked up the phone and I said, in Ukrainian,

"Hello, is this Olexa Popadenko?"

"Da," answering "Yes" in Russian.

I wondered if this person was truly my dad and asked if he could speak Ukrainian. His response was,

"Tak." "Yes" in Ukrainian. I continued,

"I am calling from Calgary, Canada. My name is Lesia Popadenko. I believe I am your daughter."

"I don't believe so because my two daughters and wife died during the war," he replied.

"Was your wife's name Tamara and your two daughters Halyna and Olesia?" I asked.

"Yes, but they died in a train explosion. My wife had just remarried and was leaving Ukraine shortly before her death. Her new name was Prychodko."

"Daddy, that was us! We didn't die. We were able to jump off the train before it exploded."

"But I was there. When I found out that you were on that train, a friend of mine, who also had his family on that train, travelled with me to catch up with you. When we got to the train, it was already blown up. My friend found his dead wife and children, but there were so many bodies and body parts that could not be identified, I assumed that you belonged to all those unidentifiable dead."

"But how is it that you are alive? We received word that you died when you were sent to fight in the war? What happened with you?"

"Well, we were fighting the Germans in Poland. Those Nazis wiped out our whole unit. I was on a horse. When I was shot and fell wounded off my horse, the dead horse fell on top of me. Later, when all the

116

bodies were collected and the dead horse removed off me, someone noticed that I may still be alive. I was taken to a hospital and stayed there a very long time before I was healed. A Russian doctor there, Nina Shevko, took good care of me. Finally, when I was able to leave the hospital, I couldn't find you. I started searching through the Red Cross and eventually got word that you were on that train."

"Dad, we definitely were on that train. I remember it very clearly. I am your little girl, Dzyoun. I know it for sure now. I will write and send you pictures of you and me. Mom and Halia died a long time ago. Halia died in Germany in 1947 and mom died in Canada in 1949. But I am very well and have three lovely daughters, so you're a grandfather."

I began sending my dad letters and old pictures, describing my life and my desire to be reunited with him. His first letter to me began with the words,

My Beloved Daughter!

I cannot express the joy those precious words meant for me. My darling daddy was back. The love I felt from him in the past penetrated throughout my whole body, as I kept reading those three words. Those words generated warmth, affection, desire, and were all aimed solely at me. It was as if once again I became my daddy's little girl and he became my loving father. Oh God, how wonderful I felt. It was a miracle that I finally reconnected to the family I had lost. I so desperately wanted to be near him and wanted to touch him. I needed to show him that I had always loved him and still did.

As it became increasingly important for me to find a way to see my dad, I began to investigate if it would be possible. My worry, which I shared with my daughters, was that I may not be able to return to Canada from Russia because of my secret escape from Soviet Ukraine. With all my different names and documents, I could have problems coming back. To guarantee my safety, I made sure that my passport had all the names, Hawrelak, Popadenko, Prychodko, and that I also was in possession of my Canadian citizenship papers. I was glad that I got my citizenship as soon as I turned twenty-one years old. I remember having to answer questions about Canada. There was one particular question,

What can you tell me about the Eskimos?

I was very pleased to answer that question because I had just heard that the Eskimos in Edmonton had won the football game. When I told the judge about the game, his response displayed a big smile and he said,

"I'm sure you'll make a very good Canadian cheering for our team."

I guess it did not matter to him that I went off the topic.

With all my documents, I also needed a Russian invitation from my dad to procure travel forms for

Soviet Russia because I was not travelling as a tourist. This later prompted the Canadian Security Intelligence Service to investigate me after my return to Canada to ensure I was not a spy. I was asked if I had picked up a Russian lover, one trained to spy by attaching himself to the unmarried Canadian woman. By answering, "No, I did not" and giving CSIS all my names, phone numbers, dates, and places from my contact in Russia, I was cleared of any espionage.

October 2, 1988, I flew KLM from Calgary to Amsterdam and changed planes to Aeroflot for my flight to Leningrad. My flight aboard KLM was very pleasant but once I entered the Aeroflot plane I noticed cramped, soiled seats. The flight attendant was most disorganized and demanded we sit in empty seats, ignoring our assigned boarding passes. People were bumping into one another before everyone could settle down. Soon I could hear the sound of Russian Gypsy music resonating throughout the plane. I like Gypsy music and began convincing myself to enjoy the domestic style of flying and not lose sight of the importance of my trip.

We landed in Leningrad late afternoon and I saw soldiers with guns standing around the plane. I became uncomfortable remembering my childhood fear of soldiers. After being ushered to the Immigration and Customs area, I showed all my documents that had to match all of my dad's confirmation for my special arrival. Because I was returning to the USSR country of my birth, I needed various documents to be able to stay in my father's private residence. Once cleared with Immigration, my experience with the Customs people was as I had expected. When I opened my luggage and the officer tumbled through everything seeing a man's new winter parka I bought for my dad, he quickly said,

"You will need to pay duty on this."

That was my cue for bribery. I immediately pulled out new cassette tapes and offered candy and gum to him. He took my gifts and said,

"Go now, there is no duty imposed."

After leaving the security area, I saw five people coming towards me. Three men, one old nasty looking woman with a cane, and also a bit younger, pleasant woman holding a round, twisted bread *(kalach)* placed on an embroidered towel with a dried maple leaf stuck into the middle of the bread. I desperately searched for my dad but did not see him.

Where was dad and which of the two women was my stepmother?

One of the three men, a good looking Slavko Popadenko, was my first cousin. The old woman with a cane was my stepmother, Dr. Nina Shevko, the doctor who took care of my wounded father during the war. The other three people were her patients who had recovered from throat surgery. They chose to stay with her as she was injured with a broken ankle. I shook hands with everyone and thanked her for the special welcoming bread. I noticed the angry look on my

120

stepmother's face as if I was not welcome. She stared at me for a long time and then finally spoke briefly, in Russian, explaining that dad was in the hospital and we would see him tomorrow. That was all.

Silently, we walked outside the building with Slavko carrying my suitcase. One of the men was our taxi driver, Vadim, for the next two days. We all piled into an old Lada car and drove through the streets of the famous city of Leningrad. Everyone remained quiet and I wondered what was in store for me with these strange people.

After more than one hour, we arrived at a residential district where a whole series of identical ten-story buildings stood side by side; Stalin's version of apartment buildings. Once inside the apartment, a bad smell greeted us. Clutter was seen everywhere due to no closets for storage. The space on the right side was the living/sleeping/eating area and the left side had a small kitchen, a tiny toilet cubicle similar to a public toilet stall, and a small room containing a bathtub and a sink. The tub was completely filled with clothes, bedding, and whatever else, but at least a person could gain access to use the sink. The most disgusting place was the toilet. On each side of it were two boxes on the floor filled with potatoes, carrots, and onions covered with dish towels. The stench was unbearable. With no window and no ventilation, the leftover odors of human waste mixed with stored veggies created a choking atmosphere. When I entered and turned on the light switch, immediately, at least a dozen cockroaches scattered in different directions. I almost fainted and at the same time was wondering how two educated, responsible citizens could live in such filthy surroundings; stepmother Nina, a doctor, a surgeon; dad, a professor, a war hero who became a colonel in the army.

Inside the apartment, all six of us crowded around the table in the living room area where the pleasant woman, Elsa, prepared food and drinks ahead of time. Everyone spoke Russian and I was able to respond in Russian as well. (I remembered some Russian from childhood and also had taken courses in Russian at the University of Calgary as options for my degree.) The food was tasty and the drinks were straight and unending. My stepmother proceeded to drink excessively and started boasting about her accomplishments in life, praising the likes of Lenin, and using swear words. She insisted I call her mama Nina and continued drinking. I could not believe how much this woman drank. I lied and said I could not drink much because of a sore stomach, but thanked her for offering. It was getting very late, so everyone left except for my cousin who came from Ukraine to be with me.

For sleeping arrangements, this mama Nina said she slept on the sofa these days so I could have dad's bed and my cousin slept on a cot beside the window. There were piles of newspapers, extra bedding, clothes, and many pillows on dad's bed. She pushed everything off the bed down to the floor, straightened the pillows, sprinkled perfume on what looked like soiled linen and said,

"Now you can sleep like a queen sunk into these lovely pillows!"

The lights were turned off and, lying in the dark, I wondered if all this was a bad dream. I immediately became aware that something was crawling around me. From the moon reflection in the window, I could see several cockroaches coming out of the woodwork everywhere; on the table, the walls, the floor, and on my bed.

What was I to do? I must not panic.

I started reassuring myself that these bugs were harmless and, since the people here had survived them, so could I. But, I did insert some tissue into my ears to prevent anything crawling there and covered most of my face with the blanket. I didn't sleep much that night, worrying about those ugly critters appearing on my face and scalp.

Bed.

123

Morning came and I was exhausted, not just from a sleepless night but also from the long traveling time and the emotional tension. It was good for me to have my cousin around. He was friendly and I could communicate with him in Ukrainian. I had brought one of my mom's poems and whispered to him if I should show it to my dad. All of a sudden, I heard a loud scream from the cooking area where my stepmother Nina was yelling that we were talking behind her back. This woman became hysterical. She yelled at me with such anger that I thought she was going to hit me. It did not make any sense, so I ignored her rage and decided to apologize to ease the situation for our visit to the hospital. Days later, I learned that she wanted to have children of her own but dad would not allow bringing children into this chaotic world that swallowed up his two little girls. And now, here I was; his own daughter. Apparently, she had many abortions.

Vadim, our trusty taxi driver, showed up in the morning and we were off to see my dad. On the way there, stepmother Nina said that dad would have a blood transfusion in the next day and that she had already paid for a healthy teenage girl. I volunteered to be a donor if my blood was compatible with his but she said I was too old. She said that a healthy girl was coming to the hospital to lie down beside dad and be directly connected to him. I was very surprised at such procedure because I regularly donated blood with the Red Cross and could not imagine a transfusion from a physically connected person. Thinking of Canada, I did appreciate our free blood transfusions.

We arrived at the hospital; a very old, run down building which, by our standards in Canada, would be condemned. We were going to take the elevator to the seventh floor but it was out-of-order, so we walked up. My heart started beating faster with anticipation of meeting my father. We reached his room and opened the door. There he was; dressed, clean shaven, sitting on the bed. This was my wonderful daddy. Everything about his looks appealed to me and I noticed some resemblance to me. He was old but distinguished with a certain kindness and gentleness about him. I wanted to shout aloud with joy. I wanted him to take me in his arms and call me his little girl. But nothing came out of his mouth and there was no movement from his body. He sat on the bed motionless. I approached him, hugged him, and kissed him. He responded gently to my touch as I sat beside him. My stepmom Nina, who sat at the little table by the window, said that they were leaving. Vadim took pictures of us and they all departed. The door closed, and I was left alone with my dad at last.

Dad with me on the bed, stepmother Nina and cousin Slavko, October 4, 1988.

I had to pinch myself to believe that I was in the presence of my beloved father. I started asking all kinds of questions about him, about me, about our lives in general. He answered all my questions but did not volunteer to say anything beyond that. I tried reaching his soul on a very personal level but he was somewhat distant. Then I began talking about the horrors of war and how Ukrainians were forced to flee their own country. I was surprised that he said German repression of Ukraine was worse than the Soviet regime and wondered if he had succumbed to Soviet brainwashing. Had he? He was working and lecturing in Russia after WWII and was married to a Russian doctor. He had become a colonel, a war hero, after recovering from his injuries and staying away from active duty. Could he be a communist? Looking at this gentle, frail person, I could only see my daddy and decided to leave all my worries of political affairs unresolved. It was finally time for me to rejoice in our reunion and not erase the special love for the lost father I missed all my life. But, I still had to hear his reaction to the possibility of Ukraine's independence. So I asked for an answer. Quietly, he said,

"My dear daughter, it is impossible for Ukraine to be independent because she is like the most beautiful, desirable woman in the whole world who is admired and lusted by all. It is better that she is ruled by the Russians who are her neighbours than by some other foreign country like Germany. Look how throughout history Ukraine was always conquered by foreign invaders because of her wealth and beauty."

I agreed with him that Ukraine had rich natural resources, being the second largest country next to Russia in the USSR, and feeding about half of their fifteen Soviet Union nations. What I opposed was Russia's superiority in spreading propaganda about Ukraine being nothing more than little Russia and, especially, destroying the spirit of Ukrainian people. We continued talking about Ukraine's patriotism and I kept expressing my disappointment about the existence of the Soviet Union and the Kremlin's inhuman control over its people. He agreed with me about all of Stalin's cruelty and said that the USSR badly needed domestic improvement. He concluded by saying he believed living under a socialist government was much better than living under capitalism. No more was said and I assumed he was either too ill to care about politics or became very cautious of his present surroundings. He seemed to be somewhat insecure. Although I was disappointed with our conversation, I immediately realized that the door to dad's room was wide open and a nurse had entered inside the room with lunch for both him and for me.

Fish soup and mashed potatoes with a hamburger patty. The soup tasted like dish water, the potato was bland mashed with water, and the meat reminded me of the shoe sole that Charlie Chaplin ate in his movie. After lunch, I had to leave the hospital and was disappointed with the reunion. Somehow I felt unfulfilled and walked away hungry for his affection and for some reassurance that he missed me and that he was glad to see me.

The following day, my stepmother said dad would be released from the hospital for three days and we would all go to his *dacha* (summer place) in Repin by the ocean. I decided to become very pleasant to her and offered to help with whatever housework and any cooking preparations that were needed. She seemed pleased with my offer and proceeded to give me and my cousin enough work that lasted for the next few hours. After my cousin and I finished all the work, she wanted to lie down and have a nap, so Slavko and I went out for the afternoon. He took me to the famous museum, the Hermitage, formerly the Winter Palace, the place of priceless art and history of the world culture. There was a long lineup to get inside. Slavko took me through the back door for free with no delays. The place was magnificent, filled with gold and a wealth of great works of art. Later we went for a walk and stopped at a coffee shop. We sat down by a window overlooking a canal. Slavko said to me,

"You know, this is where Dostoeyvski wrote Crime and Punishment. And did you know that Pushkin was killed right outside this coffee shop? Something to do with a lover's quarrel."

How surreal and exciting! I read their books. We sat and drank our coffee as I calmed my mind and watched the people in the street.

The next day, dad came home from the hospital and we immediately all left for his summer place by the ocean in Repin. I found Repin to be a lovely place and hoped to spend more time with dad there. I saw nice, clean apartment buildings spread among trees and grassy pathways. My cousin and I were told to go out for a walk because Elsa and my stepmother were going to prepare dinner. I enjoyed our walk and saw couples strolling hand-in-hand. The smell of fresh sea air was invigorating. We came upon an old house that once was the residence for 18th and 19th century artists and writers. We went inside the house and I stood next to the famous original painting by artist Repin in 1891; "Zaporizhian Cossaks are writing a letter to the Turkish sultan."

When we returned to the apartment, the table was full of food and liquor. As we started eating and drinking, my stepmother began talking about her achievements as a doctor and how she dedicated her whole life to taking care of my dad. Again she kept praising herself and her life's devotion to keeping my father alive. The more she drank, the more she boasted. Then she started talking about my mother. She said,

"I can't believe what that mother of yours did. She couldn't wait long enough to leave your father and find herself a new husband. Shame on her for not wanting to wait long enough for a more definite proof of his death. Look at this lovely man, your father."

She continued insulting my mother until I could not keep quiet any longer and said,

"You should not talk about my mother like that. She did what she thought was best at the time. She had two little children and she was told her husband was dead. It's not nice to talk about the dead like that."

Well, what happened next was beyond belief. This woman started yelling and screaming at me with such anger that I had never experienced before.

"You fascist bitch! You talk to me like this? How dare you? You know who I am? Where is my uniform? Wait, I'll put it on and you take a picture and give it to your children. Show them who I am. Show them that I'm a celebrated doctor who was honoured for bravery with many medals. How dare you oppose me in front of your father. Apologize right now!"

Well, I could not believe what was happening. Here I was an honest fifty year old woman being treated like some immature spoiled brat. What was I to do? I turned to my dad and said,

"Dad, what do you want me to do? You know it's not my fault. What's wrong with her?"

Dad bent his head slightly and whispered to me softly,

"Honey, she's had too much drink and sugar. She's diabetic and doesn't know what she's saying. Please, for my sake, apologize to her. You see, you'll be gone soon and I will remain with her. I must please her because without her help I would have been dead long ago. She has taken good care of me over the years and I am grateful to her."

Yes, I would honour my father's request. I started apologizing to her and said I was very sorry. She responded by yelling,

"Get down on your knees!"

Silently, I kept telling myself that I would do this for my dad's benefit, even though she was one of the most despicable women I had ever met. For my daddy's sake, I got down to my knees and begged for forgiveness. I kissed her hands and forced myself to hug her ugly body. I acted like a sweet twelve year old little girl. I flattered her and added that perhaps my rudeness was a result of growing up in Canada, where there may be a different type of discipline. Anything to calm down this detestable woman.

Here we are after my apology: Dad, Slavko, Elsa, Nina and me.
(Taxi driver, Vadim, who stayed for dinner, took the picture and then left.)

Finally, she settled down, and I stepped outside with my cousin. What was I to do next? I knew that dad had to go back to the hospital and Slavko was returning to Ukraine. I could not imagine tolerating another eight days with this woman. I asked my cousin if he could take me to Ukraine for a few days. He said he would but we'd need to come up with a good reason for doing so. I thought of a reason. We went back inside and I said to my dad,

"Dad, will you give me permission to go to Kyiv for a few days with Slavko so that I could pick up some Ukrainian soil and bring it for my daughters in Canada? I can also bring you some Ukrainian newspapers, as Slavko mentioned that you enjoy reading them and they're not available in Russia. I know that you are returning to the hospital tomorrow but I'll be back to spend more time with you."

I put forth my best charm for both dad and his wife and it worked. I received my permission and the next day, dad returned to the hospital, and Slavko and I were on our way to Ukraine.

Because our train to Kyiv was leaving in the evening, Slavko and I decided to stop at the hospital to say goodbye to dad. We took two subway trains, on the way bought some fresh flowers and, while Slavko waited outside, I ran up to the 7th floor to surprise dad. He was not in his room, so I searched and found him sitting with other old men watching TV. When I spotted him with his back to me, I gently put my arm on his shoulder, leaned over, and kissed his cheek. He looked up and displayed the most loving smile, just the way I had always hoped. He appeared excited and happy to see me. He stood up and proudly told the men that I was his daughter from Canada. He seemed very alive, affectionate, and totally different from the lifeless creature I experienced before. He took my hand and we walked into the corridor discussing my plans for visiting Ukraine. He kissed me once, twice, and I finally experienced the fatherly love I had missed so much for so long. He guided me to the elevator giving me a big, gentle hug. As I left the building, I ran outside and looked up to the window of his room. There he was. Standing at the window with his hands stretched out, he was waving both hands and throwing kisses to me. I shall never forget that moment. I was his true little girl again and he was my loving father.

Slavko lived with his wife and son in Chernivtsi, Western Ukraine. His deceased parents had a duplex in Kyiv that was vacant. Slavko bought two tickets and we hopped on the train, ignoring my lack of proper documents. We reached this place in the morning after traveling all night from Leningrad. I spent three days in Kyiv, with Slavko showing me all the beautiful places that have made this grandiose city a historical cite. Unfortunately, I sensed a lack of national Ukrainian identity and heard more Russian spoken on the street than Ukrainian. Thinking back to Stalin's quest for Russification, I hoped that he did not entirely succeed. I still believed that Ukrainians living in rural areas and those in Western Ukraine, which was not part of USSR before 1945, had kept our Ukrainian language alive.

When it was time for me to go back, I wondered about my long domestic train ride which I had no legal right to be on. I had no visa and no documents for travel outside Leningrad. Slavko took me to the train station, said goodbye, and I was faced with an unforeseen risk-taking adventure. Luckily, I had a compartment with a young Russian woman who was a real estate lawyer. The other two bunk beds were empty and I was glad to share the whole space with her and practice my Russian. I could not sleep. The whistle kept blowing repeatedly and the train was stopping continually. At all the stops, I could see many people, especially women and children, running towards the train carrying all sorts of things for sale. There were handmade toys, canned and fresh vegetables and fruit, also some drinks and lots of fresh mushrooms. These people must have been waiting for trains and inhaling toxic fumes all through the night. I thought of my life in Canada and thanked God I was only a visitor.

I arrived in Leningrad without any problems and was met by the taxi man, Vadim. At home, dad was already there from the hospital to spend the next three days with me. Once again, I noticed his demeanour of indifference to my arrival and realized it was due to his wife's presence. So, I decided to revert to being that polite young girl in order to make the next three days pleasant and peaceful. I was going to make my dad's life easier, ignoring my dislike for his wife. I was going to overwhelm this woman with my undivided attention and kindness. Thus, I began calling her mama and started flattering her intelligence for being such an accomplished doctor and a war hero. I thanked her for taking very good care of my dad for so many years. I thanked her for her generosity in allowing me to visit them in their home. By evening time, she actually started liking me and began showing pictures of their younger years, one where they celebrate a wedding anniversary.

Dad and stepmom Nina dancing in 1982.

For sleeping arrangements, stepmother Nina wanted me to sleep on dad's bed with him because she said it was the nicest place. Thus, when the lights were turned off, I found myself beside my dad next to the wall and covered with my own blanket. In the still of the night, with the lights turned off, dad reached out for my hand and whispered softly,

135

"Where is that little hand that wrote letters to me from Canada?"

He took my hand gently inside his and held it close to his heart. We laid breathing quietly to the sound of the beating of our hearts. He held my hand and, once again, I became his loving daughter. Then slowly, we both fell peacefully asleep together. This time, I even forgot about all those ugly, crawling cockroaches.

Amazingly, my stepmother became very friendly towards me and actually wanted me to see some of the beautiful city of Leningrad. She asked Elsa, the nice woman who was always helping my stepmother, to show me around. I was glad to go out with Elsa because I liked this pleasant, attractive, middle-aged, single woman. We took the train and arrived in the Petrodvorets where lavish statues and waterfalls were glimmering in real gold. We walked through the peaceful, attractive parks, and then stopped at the edge overlooking the ocean where Elsa pointed to Finland. She commented that Finland's government was complaining about the pollution in those waters created by Russia. We returned to the downtown Leningrad very quickly by taking a hovercraft and then transferring to a bus. Because Leningrad had more than sixty museums and approximately one hundred monuments dedicated to the great Russia, Elsa and I chose to stop our touring and go to her place for tea. Elsa lived alone and her place was very clean, tidy, and orderly. When our conversation touched upon the subject of female hygiene, she said she had never seen a sanitary napkin and was quite surprised to hear of such luxury for women. My memory immediately flashed back forty years to my mother and her soiled rags. In my astonishment of hearing Elsa talk about her present condition, I decided to give her all my Kotex pads, panties, bras, toothpaste, and brush; all the things she could not get easily in Russia.

Elsa brought me home and left because my stepmom said the doctor was coming to the house to examine dad. I quickly started to help clean the place and put away all the liquor. When the doctor arrived, I had to leave the room but later when she left, I said to dad,

"Was that a real doctor or an intern? She was so young and beautiful."

Dad smiled and answered,

"Yes, she's a real doctor. She's Jewish and so are most of our doctors. You know, all Jews have great respect for education. Jewish children study hard and achieve good results, giving them successful careers and improved lifestyles, regardless of the countries they live in."

I agreed with dad because I remembered reading, many years ago, that Israel's population had 98 percent university graduates. I am not sure of the statistics today.

Later that day, after having tidied the place, we began cooking because stepmother Nina had invited two interesting women for dinner; one an opera singer and the other involved with some cultural events. When they arrived, they apologized for being away during my visit, thus unable to show me around their famous city. I was also a bit disappointed about that but at least I did see some of it with my cousin Slavko and Elsa. It would have been nice to see a ballet, but I was ready to go home. I was ready to go back to my safe, stable, peaceful country of Canada where I would be reunited with my daughters and would continue living a comfortable, stress-free life. Again we had drinks and everyone was wishing all kinds of toasts. When my turn came up, I stood up and said,

"I wish to thank mama Ninochka for her hospitality and ask forgiveness for any misunderstandings that I may have caused here. If I behaved in a way that may have offended anyone, I do apologize. I want you to know that I cannot be a bad person because the blood that flows in my veins is also the blood of my father. And you all know what a wonderful, honourable man he is, so some of it must surely be in me as well."

Before I could finish talking, I saw my dad was looking at me with the most pleasing expression. He gently moved his chair, slowly got up, and walked over to me. He put his arms around me in a loving embrace and held me tight. That special moment will stay with me forever because, once again, I found myself in the arms of my beloved dad and, at that exact significant, emotional time, I became fully aware that I was no longer an orphan.

My daddy and me in 1988.

The next morning I was taken to the airport, carrying a *samovar* (electric urn used to boil water for tea in Russia), a present from mama Nina. I also carried a religious picture of Ukraine's 1000 year anniversary of Christianity I had bought in Kyiv. I said good-bye to my dad, hugged him, and told him I loved him. I wanted to bring him to Canada, if only for a visit, but he declined and repeatedly kept saying that he was too old and too weak to travel. I waived to him smiling, throwing kisses, and then slowly disappeared into the restricted area of the airport.

Leningrad airport, saying goodbye to dad and mama Nina.

When I finally arrived in our beautiful Canada and was going through the Immigration in Calgary, the Immigration Officer said to me,

"So, how did you like Russia?"

To that I quickly replied,

"If you ask me to get down on my knees and kiss the floor I'm standing on, I will do it. I am so glad to return home to Canada!"

CONCLUSION

It has been twenty-six years since my dad and I found one another after being separated during World War II. Sadly, he died seven months after my visit, at the age of 81. I received a postcard from stepmother Nina, hand written by Elsa, that dad passed May 1, 1989. He was buried in the Repin cemetery outside St. Petersburg. That was all. Following dad's death, I had no more contact with his wife. I learned later that she also died shortly after dad. Although my cousin, Slavko Popadenko, visited me in Canada in the fall of 1989, he returned to Soviet Ukraine and I presume died some years later as well because I have not heard from him since 1997. Thus, my connection to family members left me as quickly as it appeared. I am grateful for having had those special moments with my wonderful, gentle father where I resurrected those precious feelings I once shared with him as a child. I am sure it meant the same for him. The reunion also provided answers to a number of questions I had about my past, and gave me positive reinforcement on the successful life I was leading with my daughters in Canada.

1991 brought an incredible event for Ukraine. Independence! More than 90 percent of Ukrainian citizens voted for independence from the Soviet Union. A chairman was elected, Leonid Kravchuk, as the President of Ukraine. Then a meeting was held where the presidents of Ukraine, Belarus and Russia officially dissolved Soviet Union and formed the Commonwealth of Independent States. The Soviet Union ceased to exist in December 1991. Ukraine became independent and its true blue-and-yellow flag was resurrected in January 1992. Oh, if only my mother, my father, and my two stepfathers were alive to see it for themselves. Years ago, my first stepfather, Mykola Prychodko, expressed it in his publication, "Ukraine and Russia" (Winnipeg: New Pathway, 1953, p. 22) as,

...We also pray that Ukraine may soon break away from the Russian prison of nations and becomes one of a family of free nations....

Most of my parents' generation of Ukrainians who came to Canada after World War II to avoid Soviet tyranny wished for such a glorious event and hoped that someday it would be possible to return to their free native country. None of them believed that such a miracle was probable because, for years, Russia's evil domination trampled Ukraine with intimidation and oppression by trying to kill its existence as a unique country. Today, we are able to acknowledge that Ukraine is a separate, distinct country, and that its people have survived the injustice and the suffering imposed upon them. Ukrainians are the people who have never lost their Ukrainian identity, in Ukraine and abroad. Although the country has finally emerged as an independent nation, there are still many unresolved political and economic issues. Hopefully, Ukraine will get rid of any wrongdoing and corruption that was carried over by leaders of Soviet Ukraine, and its people will be able to enjoy living in their country of restored economic wealth and political freedom.

In the past ten years, I have visited Ukraine twice. I took my three daughters to visit Kyiv in 2004. Our trip also included a stop at Mittenwald, Germany to see my old refugee camp which is now a German army base.   In Mittenwald we spent some time at the cemetery where my sister Halia was buried. Her grave was no longer there, as someone else was put in her place, due to the fee for the burial plot not being paid. In 2012, I joined a lovely tour of Ukraine where I was able to meet Ukrainian citizens, enjoy seeing beautiful landscapes and historical architecture. Although I found that people of Western Ukraine spoke the Ukrainian language everywhere, in Kyiv, the capital of Ukraine, I did hear Russian spoken on the street, in some hotels and restaurants. Sadly, I concluded that such a lack of the Ukrainian language was a direct result of the powerful Soviet control forbidding the use of the Ukrainian language in Eastern Ukraine. And, of course, there are many ethnic Russians living in the eastern part of Ukraine as well.

My daughters and me on our trip to Ukraine in 2004.
Jen, Kathy, Tammy and me.

2014 saw the Russian Government perform a heinous act of ruthlessly attacking Ukrainian people and Ukrainian territory. I was horrified. How is this possible within co-operative, international laws of the twenty-first century? And then, my thoughts turned back to the tragic lives of Ukrainians during Russian oppression; before World War II, during World War II, and now. Today, Putin's Russia used false arguments insisting that Ukrainians are harming the safety of Russian speaking citizens in Ukraine. What nonsense! There has been no indication or evidence of any such violation. It is Putin who has created Russia as a state of criminal regime by using force in annexation of Crimea. Crimea was secured within Ukraine's peaceful territory in 1994. It was the agreement with Russia, Great Britain, United States, and Ukraine where Ukraine got rid of all its nuclear weapons and gave them to Russia. In return, Ukraine was promised to preserve its territorial integrity and respect for its borders and political freedom. Unfortunately, Putin disregards this international law and, after unlawfully occupying Crimea, he continues his brutal, illegal invasion of Eastern Ukraine. I hope the free countries of the Western world will provide international help and support to stop Russia from interfering with Ukraine's transition for an improved, democratic existence. I pray that the fighting in Eastern Ukraine comes to a complete stop, where thousands of innocent people are being wounded and killed under Putin's leadership.

I have not forgotten my childhood turmoil of war, poverty, and a life as an orphan. Yet, in spite of all obstacles in my youth, I have always maintained a positive outlook on my life. I am grateful to be the daughter of wonderful, smart, caring, parents who, unfortunately, left me at a very early age, but whose loving memory stayed with me forever. I believe that my interaction with stepfathers and stepmothers also contributed to my maturity which resulted in my ability to experience contentment and joy. I have been fortunate to live in this wonderful, democratic country of Canada which allows me to keep my Ukrainian identity. Ukraine is the place where I was born and the country I shall cherish forever. Canada has been my home for sixty-seven years, and that's where I want to remain to the end.

After all these years and knowledge gained, my fear of the dead still lingers. When I came to Canada, I brought with me the small Christmas decoration that mom made for me in 1946. I misplaced it quite some time ago and had given up hope of ever finding it in my home. On my seventy-fifth birthday, I had an interesting dream. My mom came to visit me and I told her to go away because she was dead and I was afraid. She smiled at me while standing in front of a small bookcase in my bedroom. A few days after my dream, I had a new furnace installed which required moving the same bookcase from my dream. To my amazement, hiding behind it was my mom's missing ornament. I cannot help thinking that my mom was guiding me to this lost treasure, although my fear of the dead was reaffirmed.

Today, I am retired on a University of Calgary Academic Pension and have good health to enjoy my daughters' families. I love my daughters with all my heart. I love my grandchildren and feel very close to them and to their fathers. I am also fortunate to share many family celebrations with my ex-husband, Michael, and his lovely wife, Sandi. My senior years have allowed me the freedom to experience international travel both independently and with my family. I have enjoyed hiking, skiing and snow shoeing in the mountains, along with many activities that include my grandchildren. My life is currently at its best, having gone from an orphan to a loving family of twelve. I can honestly say that my life has been filled with many adventures, education, family, friends, and, above all, love.

Printed in Canada